Praise for *The Language of E*

"Emotional awareness can be your biggest superpower. In this workbook, Karla McLaren offers powerful exercises that will help you understand your emotions and tap into their wisdom. With Karla as your guide, you'll dig deep and explore your own endlessly fascinating inner world."

DEBBIE SORENSEN, PHD
author of *ACT for Burnout*

"Accessing the wisdom of our emotions is key to understanding ourselves and making better decisions. This brilliant workbook offers readers a set of easy-to-follow practices to help them receive the precious gifts and skills in their emotions."

VERED KOGAN
host of *The Mindset Game* podcast and CEO of the Momentum Institute

"The genius of Karla McLaren's latest book can be summed up by three sentences in her introduction: 'Your emotions don't create problems. They arise to help you deal with problems. Learn their language, and you can change your life.' Without a doubt, this is THE workbook for better mental health, relationships that flourish, and overall life success and satisfaction."

ANITA NOWAK, PHD
author of *Purposeful Empathy*

"The beauty of this workbook is how it orients you back to yourself, with questions and exercises designed to help you meet yourself with more understanding and acceptance. Karla McLaren's work reminds us that emotions exist because we need them, and that if we learn their language, we can revolutionize our emotional intelligence and transform our relationships. Use this workbook and you'll become a healthier you."

MICHAEL T. MCRAY
founder of Becoming Restored and author of *I Am Not Your Enemy*

The
LANGUAGE
of
EMOTIONS
Workbook

Also by Karla McLaren

The
LANGUAGE
of
EMOTIONS
Workbook

A Practical Guide
to Reveal the Wisdom
in Each of Your Feelings

KARLA McLAREN, M.Ed.

Sounds True
Boulder, CO

This book is not intended as a substitute for the medical recommendations of physicians, mental health professionals, or other health-care providers. Rather, it is intended to offer information to help the reader cooperate with physicians, mental health professionals, and health-care providers in a mutual quest for optimal well-being. We advise readers to carefully review and understand the ideas presented and to seek the advice of a qualified professional before attempting to use them.

Published 2024

Cover design by Charli Barnes
Book design by Linsey Dodaro

Printed in Canada

BK07090

ISBN 9781649633330 (paperback) | ISBN 9781649633347 (ebook)

Contents

Hello Reader!

I'm glad you're here, and I'm glad to welcome you to the magnificent world of emotions. I've been exploring, studying, researching, and working with the amazing intelligence inside the emotions for many decades, and I'm happy to share their wise and healing nature with you.

However, I understand that you may not think of emotions in this way. You may have experienced emotions as problems, either in yourself or in the behavior of others. You may have learned that certain emotions are negative and unnecessary or that other emotions are positive and should be felt as often as is humanly possible.

But if you're like most of us, you haven't learned the most important things:

1. What emotions are

2. Why emotions arise

3. How emotions work

4. How to work with all emotions skillfully

Most of us have had a very poor emotional education, and when emotions are present, we often don't know what to do. Even in our everyday language, you can see that we don't really know how to connect with emotions in ways that work.

For instance, when you think of the word *emotional*, what comes to mind? Are emotional people deeply wise, or are they irrational? Are they grounded and focused, or are they unstable? Are emotional people trustworthy, or do you want to distance yourself from them?

 When you or others are called **emotional**, what does that mean? Take a moment to jot down some of the qualities an emotional person might possess.

For most of us, the word *emotional* has a negative meaning, and when we call someone (or ourselves) emotional, it's not a compliment! The experience of feeling and displaying emotions has been turned into a problem, and that's not helpful to anyone, because emotions are vital parts of our ability to think, decide, act, dream, and love. Emotions are essential to our ability to relate to ourselves, to others, and to the world around us.

And this word *emotional* is pretty sloppy, because we may not even know which emotions we're talking about. Are we noticing anger in emotional people, or are we seeing sadness, joy, anxiety, envy, panic, happiness, or shame? Which emotions are present, or does it even matter?

Actually, it matters a lot because emotions are a necessary part of everything you are.

Understanding Emotions Is Essential to Your Health and Well-Being

Every thought, every choice, every relationship, every dream, every failure, every triumph, every decision, and every action you take is directed by your emotions. Because of this, understanding them and learning their language is essential.

And here's the most remarkable thing: your emotions are not problems! Your emotions arise to help you *deal with* problems, and they bring you gifts and abilities such as boundary setting (anger), intuition (fear), motivation (anxiety), relaxation (sadness), and healthy self-esteem (contentment).

Each of your emotions contains wisdom, benefits, and skills that you can't get anywhere else, and each of them is important. When you can learn the language of your emotions, you can change your life.

Welcome to *The Language of Emotions Workbook*!

This workbook complements my book *The Language of Emotions*, and it explores seventeen unique emotions and the Empathic Mindfulness practices that come from my applied work, which is called Dynamic Emotional Integration® (or DEI for short).

With these ideas and practices, you can learn how to access the information and intelligence inside each of your emotions. This workbook also includes self-care and communication practices to help you develop a healthy emotional life, healthy relationships, and healthy empathy.

How to Use This Workbook

This workbook is yours to use in whatever ways work for you. You can read through from beginning to end and complete each of the activities and reflections, or you can skip around based on your needs and interests.

I've created many different ways for you to understand and work with your emotions, including questions, exercises, mindfulness practices, and art practices. Of course, if a specific way of engaging with this workbook works best for you, please rely on your own way of learning.

This workbook can help you learn how to work directly with your own emotions, which are essential aspects of your deep intelligence and your capacity for healing. You'll learn to ground and focus yourself, identify and regulate your emotions, understand yourself and others more deeply, and access your own unique emotional wisdom. And, as you may already know, when you can work with your emotions, they may bring unresolved situations or wounds into your consciousness to help you address and heal them. This can be a relief, and it can also be disorienting or distressing sometimes. It's important to know that nothing is wrong with you or your emotions if this happens; this is often a sign of healing.

However, if your emotions feel overwhelming, please visit my online learning community, empathyacademy.org, and reach out to a DEI professional there, or to your local crisis hotline, your doctor, or an emotionally respectful counselor or therapist. You can also find bonus practices for this workbook at karlamclaren.com/LoE-workbook or by scanning the QR code below.

Thank you for taking this time for yourself, and thank you for bringing more emotional awareness, stronger relationships, and healthier empathy to our waiting world.

Here's to being emotional in ways that truly work!

Karla

PART 1

Introducing the Wisdom in Your Emotions

All of your emotions are essential to your well-being.

Each one brings you a specific kind of intelligence to
guide your thoughts and actions – and you can learn to
work brilliantly with every emotion you have.

What Are Emotions and Why Do They Arise?

My favorite definition of emotions comes from sociologist Arlie Russell Hochschild, who wrote this in her book *The Managed Heart*:

> *Emotion, I suggest, is a biologically given sense, and our most important one. Like other senses – hearing, touch, and smell – it is a means by which we know our relation to the world, and is therefore crucial to the survival of human beings in group life. Emotion is unique among the senses, however, because it is related not only to an orientation toward **action**, but also to an orientation toward **cognition**.*

So, emotions are senses that help you think, understand, and act. They help you know your world, and they help you make sense of what you feel and perceive.

Sensing Your Own Emotions

Your emotions help you make sense of yourself and the world, each in its own way. Your emotions are an essential part of you, and each one contains a vital piece of your intelligence and your ability to think and act.

 Think of a time when you felt joyous. What were you sensing? What was your joy telling you about the situation?

Now think of a time when you felt angry. What was your anger sensing, and what was it telling you about the situation?

Since most of us have learned that emotions are problems (or that they create problems), we can have a difficult time learning how to work with them. Luckily, your emotions are working to help you at all times, and you can learn to identify them by the skills they bring to you.

Your emotions don't **create** problems.
They arise to help you **deal with** problems.
Learn their language, and you can change your life.

Let's explore the skills and intelligence inside five of your emotions and see how you're working with them right now.

Discovering the Emotional Skills You Already Have

Each of your emotions arises for specific reasons, and each emotion brings you skills, benefits, and forms of intelligence that you can't get anywhere else. Your responses to the statements below will help you identify some of the wisdom and skills that are already working for you in five essential (but often misunderstood) emotions.

How to find your score: As you read each statement below, choose the response that describes how you feel about it and note the number associated with your response. In each subsection, you'll add up your responses to find your score for that particular emotional skill.

Higher scores for each emotion may mean that you already have access to the skills and benefits of that particular emotion, while lower scores may mean that you have some confusion about or difficulty accessing that emotion at this time.

In either case, skip forward to each emotion's section to learn more about its essential place in your life. The principles and practices in this workbook will help you develop a full range of emotional skills so that you can access the benefits and wisdom in every emotion you have.

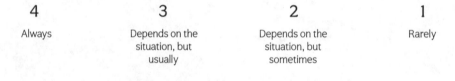

4	3	2	1
Always	Depends on the situation, but usually	Depends on the situation, but sometimes	Rarely

{ Your Emotional Skills: **Boundaries** }

1. I feel heard and respected in my
   relationships with others.   4   3   2   1

2. I am comfortable speaking up for myself,
   even during conflicts.   4   3   2   1

3. I can identify and separate my own
   emotions from the emotions of others.   4   3   2   1

Your score for questions 1-3 _____

Questions 1-3 focus on the wisdom and skills in your **ANGER**
Low Score: **3** | High score: **12**

THE HEART OF ANGER: Many of us have felt (or learned) that anger is always a problem, but at its heart, anger helps you set and restore healthy boundaries around yourself and the things that you value. Anger helps you create a private and defined space for yourself, your thoughts, your dreams and ideas, and especially your emotions.

 How easy is it for you to set clear boundaries in your relationships?

4. I have good time-management skills,
    and I follow through on my plans and   4   3   2   1
    commitments.

5. I tend to be good at organizing my ideas,   4   3   2   1
    my tasks, and my physical space.

6. When I think of large projects or places
    I have to get to at a specific time, I feel   4   3   2   1
    pretty relaxed.

Your score for questions 4–6: _____
Questions **4–6** focus on the wisdom and skills in your **ANXIETY**.
Low score: **3** | High score: **12**

THE HEART OF ANXIETY: Anxiety is nearly always presented as a negative emotion
(or even as a form of mental illness), but at its heart, anxiety helps you gather the energy
and motivation you need to plan and complete your projects and meet your deadlines.
Anxiety is a forward focused emotion that motivates and organizes you, and it's essential
for pretty much everything you do.

   How do you feel about your ability to motivate yourself and get things done?

{ Your Emotional Skills: **Instincts** }

7. I am comfortably aware of my
   surroundings, and I tend to be relaxed   4   3   2   1
   about changes.

8. I tend to remain calm and focused in   4   3   2   1
   emergencies.

9. I tend to trust my own instincts about   4   3   2   1
   what's right for me, and I act on them.

Your score for questions 7-9: _____

Questions **7-9** focus on the wisdom and skills in your **FEAR.**
Low score: **3** | High score: **12**

THE HEART OF FEAR: Fear is usually treated as a sign of cowardice, but nothing could be further from the truth. At its heart, fear contains your instincts and intuition about the present moment. Without your fear, you simply wouldn't know where you are or what's going on. Fear is a present focused emotion that can help you connect to your intuition and instincts about yourself and your world.

 How connected do you feel to your instincts and intuition?

10. I'm able to change my mind when I
discover new information and ideas.

    4   3   2   1

11. I can move on from situations that aren't
healthy or aren't working.

    4   3   2   1

12. I can relax and calm myself down, and I
have reliable self-soothing skills.

    4   3   2   1

Your score for questions 10–12: _____

Questions **10–12** focus on the wisdom and skills in your **SADNESS**.
Low score: **3** | High score: **12**

THE HEART OF SADNESS: Many people see sadness (and crying) as weakness, but I call sadness "the all-purpose healing balm of the soul." Sadness helps you let go of things that aren't working anymore. When you can let go of things (belongings, ideas, behaviors, relationships, etc.) that no longer work for you, sadness can help you relax, replenish yourself, and make room for things that *do* work.

 How do you behave when you realize that it's time to let something go?

{ Your Emotional Skills: Ethics }

13. I have a fairly easy time changing
    problem behaviors or old habits.

        4   3   2   1

14. When I make a social mistake, I can
    apologize and correct myself.

        4   3   2   1

15. I can usually ask for help and support.

        4   3   2   1

Your score for questions 13–15: _____
Questions **13–15** focus on the wisdom and skills in your **SHAME**.
Low score: **3** | High score: **12**

THE HEART OF SHAME: Shame may be one of our most hated emotions, which is a real shame, because it's essential to your ability to understand yourself and change your behaviors when you need to. Shame helps you live up to your morals and ethics, and it holds you to the standards you set for yourself. The work with shame is not to repress it when it's painful, but to question whether the standards you've set for yourself are workable and appropriate (I call these standards your *shaming messages* or your *contracts*). If the messages and contracts your shame is upholding are unworkable, the Burning Contracts practices on pages 55–58 are specific healing practices that can help you and your shame get some distance from the painful influence of these unworkable messages.

 How do you behave when you know you've made a mistake or done something you don't feel proud of?

No matter where you score right now, you can deepen your emotional skills and learn to access the wisdom in each of your emotions. These questions are a way for you to take a momentary snapshot of where you are with these five emotions, and this workbook will help you develop new skills and new ways to work with the intelligence in each of them – and in all seventeen of your emotions.

 Which of these five emotions are you most skilled with at this moment?

Which of these emotions need some support?

As you observe your high-scoring emotions, think back: Where did you learn these skills?

As you observe your lower-scoring emotions, think back: Where and how did you learn to avoid these skills?

In the following section, you'll find an alphabetized list of the gifts, skills, and wisdom your emotions contain so that you can see all of your important emotional senses in one place.

Introducing the Gifts and Skills in Your Emotions

Your emotions are vital senses that help you understand and respond to the world around you. In this alphabetized list, you'll see that each of your emotions contributes a unique set of skills and wisdom to help you make sense of your world.

ANGER supports you when you, what you value, or someone else has been challenged, and it helps you set and maintain healthy boundaries.

ANXIETY motivates you to prepare for the future and get things done well and on time.

APATHY (or boredom), as a protective mask for anger, lets you know when you're not able or willing to set clear boundaries, and it can help you get some distance from unworkable situations.

CONFUSION, as a healing mask for fear and anxiety, lets you know when there's too much going on around you or inside you, and it can give you a much-needed time out.

CONTENTMENT lets you know when you've done something well, and it helps you view yourself with pride and satisfaction.

ENVY helps you gain and maintain access to security, resources, and recognition (and support these things for others as well).

FEAR connects you to your intuition and your instincts about the present moment, and it alerts you to change, novelty, or possible hazards in your environment.

GRIEF helps you take the time to feel, remember, and honor your losses — of things, ideas, people, animals, or situations that were important to you.

HAPPINESS helps you look inside yourself, around you, and toward the future with hope and delight.

HATRED arises in the presence of the things you cannot accept in yourself (or despise in others).

JEALOUSY helps you choose and maintain strong, loyal, and supportive relationships.

JOY helps you experience inspiration and feel a blissful sense of oneness with the world.

PANIC protects you when your life is in danger and helps you heal from past traumas.

SADNESS helps you let go of things that are no longer working for you. Sadness helps you release, relax, and create space for new things that *do* work.

SHAME (or guilt) helps you choose and maintain your morals and ethics so that you don't hurt, embarrass, or dehumanize yourself or others.

SITUATIONAL DEPRESSION drains your energy to help you slow down and identify things that are not working in your life.

THE SUICIDAL URGE arises when something in your life needs to end, but it's not your actual, physical life! Reach out for help to identify the situation that needs to end so that you can get your life back. See page 136 for help and support.

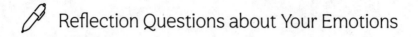 Reflection Questions about Your Emotions

Which two emotions are most comfortable for you right now?

a. Which forms of wisdom do these comfortable emotions bring to you?

b. How do you respond when these comfortable emotions arise?

Which two emotions are most challenging for you right now?

a. Which forms of wisdom do these challenging emotions bring to you?

b. How do you respond when these challenging emotions arise?

How Emotions Work
(and How to Work with Them Skillfully)

Your emotions arise in specific situations and bring you the energy and intelligence you need to respond or take action – and you have many choices for how you respond when your emotions arise.

An important part of developing emotionally intelligent responses is to understand how emotions work, and how to work with them (instead of against them).

An Immediate Emotion Pathway

In many situations you might immediately take action. In these situations, the pathway your emotions take might look something like this:

 Think of a situation where you respond swiftly. One example might be when you see someone you love and smile with happiness and joy.

What other emotions move this quickly for you? Write down a few situations and the emotions that arise to support you:

In many situations, you may feel an emotion and act instantly. Sometimes that's fine: for instance, when you smile with delight when you see a loved one.

But with some emotions, like intense anger or intense jealousy, you may act in ways that hurt you or other people. If that happens, it's essential to learn how to work with those emotions in healthier ways.

Learning to Feel and Identify Your Emotions

You can add some pauses into your emotion pathway so that you'll have the time you need to work with the wisdom your emotions contain.

The first two pauses you can add are to *feel* and *identify* your emotions: to sense them, and to identify which ones they are. When you know which emotions you're feeling, you'll understand the situation more clearly and be able to make choices about how you'll respond and act (or *not* act, sometimes).

When you add these healing pauses, your pathway will look something like this:

Situation Emotion *Feel* *Identify* Act

Feeling and identifying your emotions can help you relax and focus yourself. The Emotional Vocabulary List on pages 160-166 will help you learn more words for many different emotional states, which will help you become more skilled in these important *feeling* and *identifying* parts of your emotion pathway.

 Think of a situation where you or someone you know acted very quickly. An example might be when something frightened you, and you reacted by yelling or striking out.

What was the situation?

How strong was the emotional response?

Which emotion(s) was present?

What action was taken?

If you can slow down your emotional responses and add some supportive pauses, you'll be able to understand yourself, your emotions, and your responses more clearly.

Adding Healing Pauses to Your Emotion Pathway

As you know, emotions can contain a great deal of energy. Inserting these *feeling* and *identifying* pauses into your emotion pathway can help you harness the energy of your emotions instead of exploding with them, repressing the life out of them, or overlooking them altogether. These healthy pauses will give you more time, more space, and more focus so that you can respond mindfully and intentionally.

The next important step is to learn how to work *with* your emotions instead of working *for* them with unskilled expression or working *against* them with unhealthy repression. When you know how to work *with* your emotions, you'll be able to choose the healthiest and most appropriate actions.

When you add this *working with* pause, your pathway will look something like this:

Situation   Emotion   Feel   Identify   *Work with*   Act (or not)

Learning to work with your emotions means checking in with what your emotions are sensing and deciding which healthy actions they might require. Though you might think that these pauses will slow you down, they'll actually save you time and help you avoid the kinds of trouble people get into when they express their emotions without thinking – or when they repress them without listening to the wisdom they contain.

 Think of a time when you were able to pause and consider your emotional response to a situation and answer the following questions:

Which emotion (or emotions) were you feeling?

Which parts of the pathway above were you able to access?

How did your actions change?

Where did you learn to work with your emotions in this way?

Once you get used to adding these essential pauses
into your emotion pathway, you'll be able to feel and
respond quickly and with grounded emotional wisdom.

You may also discover that you don't need to take any action at all: for instance, when you misread the situation and react to something that didn't actually happen. When you can understand and work with your emotions, you'll have many choices for how you'll respond and act.

Practicing with Your Emotion Pathway

When you add these intentional pauses, you'll be able to develop your emotional skills and access the specific wisdom inside each and every emotion you have. It will take some practice, but your emotions can help you learn how to work with them.

One good way to practice is to imagine using this full pathway in times when you're not particularly emotionally activated. Practicing in this low-intensity state can help you build the skills you need for times when your emotions are very active.

You can do this with a situation in your life right now:

 What is the situation?

Which emotion(s) do you feel?

How strong is your emotional response?

What gifts and skills does that emotion(s) bring to you? (See "Introducing the Gifts and Skills in Your Emotions" on page 16.)

How can you work **with** that emotion(s)?

What action do you typically take when feeling this emotion?

What action would you take now that you've worked **with** your emotion(s)?

Creating pauses in your emotion pathway gives
you the space you need to access your awareness,
your skills, and the wisdom of your emotions.

The Four Keys to Emotional Genius

All of your emotions are necessary, and all of them bring you messages and skills to help you understand yourself and the world around you. I've discovered four keys to emotional genius that will help you work with your emotions in healing new ways.

The First Key: There Are No Negative Emotions *or* Positive Emotions

All of your emotions are messengers that tell you how you're feeling and what's going on. Each of your emotions has important messages for you, and each brings you the skills, awareness, and energy you need in every situation you encounter.

Although the way you work with your emotions can have positive or negative outcomes, the emotions themselves are not good or bad. All of your emotions bring you intelligence and information, and all of them can help you understand what's happening inside you and in your world. All of your emotions are necessary.

 Look at the list of emotions below, and place them in either the positive category or the negative category. Then ask yourself why you placed each emotion where you did. What makes an emotion seem positive? What makes an emotion seem negative?

ANGER ~ HAPPINESS ~ FEAR ~ ENVY ~ JOY ~ CONFUSION
HATRED ~ SADNESS ~ CONTENTMENT ~ GRIEF

Positive	Negative

Are there any situations where a supposedly positive emotion could have a negative effect?

Are there any situations where a supposedly negative emotion could have a positive effect?

The Second Key: Understand Emotional Nuance

Every emotion can arise at different levels of intensity. Emotions can arise in such a *soft* state that you and others might not even notice them. Emotions can also arise in a *medium* state, where you simply become aware of their presence. And in some situations, emotions can arise in an *intense* state, where they're very obvious to you and the people around you. Emotions arise at many levels of intensity, and you can learn how to identify and work with all of them.

For the four emotions in the table below, organize each of the emotional vocabulary words in parentheses by their strength: soft, medium, or intense. For instance, **annoyed** would be the soft form of anger, so you would place it in the **soft** column in the **anger** row.

EMOTION	SOFT	MEDIUM	INTENSE
ANGER (*Furious, annoyed, mad*)			
SADNESS (*Inconsolable, low, sad*)			
FEAR (*Watchful, afraid, petrified*)			
HAPPINESS (*Jubilant, smiling, delighted*)			

A larger and more articulate emotional vocabulary has been shown to help people develop better emotion regulation skills – all by itself – because a stronger vocabulary helps you identify more of your emotions. This is especially helpful for any emotions that tend to appear in their intense states for you right now.

You can use your emotional vocabulary to identify these emotions at their soft and medium states, which will help you develop skills when your emotions are less intense. In time, you'll gain the awareness and skills you need to work with the more intense forms of your emotions.

Think of two more emotions that tend to overwhelm you right now, and write down some words that refer to their soft and medium states (if you need some ideas, skip forward to the Emotional Vocabulary List on pages 161-166). Becoming aware of these softer states can help you begin to work with these emotions in new ways.

Emotion	Soft	Medium

The Third Key: Identify Multiple Emotions

It's normal to feel more than one emotion at the same time (think of crying with happiness or laughing when you're angry). Though there aren't many English words to describe feeling multiple emotions at once, emotions regularly work in pairs and groups.

For the situations below, identify the different emotions you might feel at the same time (you can find some great words in the Emotional Vocabulary List on pages 161-166).

Situation 1: You're at a friend's birthday party, and you saved up to buy her some T-shirts from her favorite musician's website. When she opens her present from another friend, she screams with excitement: he got her tickets to see this musician live, and they're going in a stretch limo!

 What emotions might you feel?

Situation 2: Two of your closest friends used to get along, but they haven't been talking to each other for months. However, both of them want to talk endlessly *to you* about the other person, and they both want you to take sides.

 What emotions might you feel?

With the help of these four keys, you and your emotions can begin to develop a common language and healthy new ways to work together.

The Fourth Key: Learn How to *Channel* Your Emotions

Instead of only expressing or repressing your emotions, you can learn how to *channel* them, meaning that you can listen to them, understand them, and work with them intentionally. When you know why your emotions arise and how to work with them, you'll have more options and more skills. You'll have many healthy options for every emotion you feel.

Expression and repression can be useful in many circumstances, but when you know how to work *with* your emotions, you'll have access to more and better choices, better self-awareness, and better understanding of others.

Expressing means displaying or acting out your emotions without a lot of thought.

Repressing means hiding, ignoring, or shutting down your emotions.

Channeling means listening to your emotions and working with them intentionally.

In the situations below, are you expressing, repressing, or channeling your emotions?

Situation 1: You walk into a party with a new shirt on, and two people you don't know very well laugh and make rude remarks about it. You feel hurt and angry, but you pretend not to be, and you laugh along with them.

        ○ Expressing   ○ Repressing   ○ Channeling

Situation 2: You're in a mandatory training at work, and you're bored out of your mind. You sigh, pull out your phone, and ignore everyone.

        ○ Expressing   ○ Repressing   ○ Channeling

Situation 3: You see your ex in a restaurant hugging and kissing someone, and you feel a huge wave of jealousy. You think to yourself, "Okay, it's clear that I'm not over our breakup yet, because this is too painful! I really need some help figuring out how to let go."

        ○ Expressing   ○ Repressing   ○ Channeling

Now choose your own situation, identify what you felt, and imagine how you could express, repress, and channel your own emotions.

PART 2

The Empathic Mindfulness Practices

The practices in the following sections will help you ground and focus yourself, soothe and regulate your energy levels, develop healthy empathy, and access the genius inside your emotions.

What Is an **Empathic** Mindfulness Practice?

I grew up in the yoga, mindfulness, and energy-healing communities, and I learned many good ways to relax and focus inward. But in those communities, the emotions were often treated as problems to be overcome. For instance, I was taught to calm my body and observe my emotions as they passed by. You may have learned something like this too.

 If you have a mindfulness practice, how does it invite you to treat emotions?

I had some pretty intense emotions trying to get my attention, and while calming myself was helpful sometimes, I began to realize that my emotions had something to say. Letting them pass by meant that I wasn't able to access their wisdom.

Over many years, I learned how to listen to my emotions and identify the gifts they brought, and I created a series of simple mindfulness practices that *rely* on emotions rather than trying to get them to pass by or dissolve.

The practices in this section help you ground, focus, and define yourself with the help of specific emotions, and they create a space for you and your emotions to engage with each other in healthy new ways.

Welcome to the Empathic Mindfulness practices!

Getting Grounded and Focused

Being grounded means feeling stable, calm, relaxed, focused, and integrated.

Signs of being ungrounded include forgetfulness, an inability to relax, physical and emotional tension, confusion, cycling thoughts, clumsiness, agitation, disorientation, and/or dissociation.

How to Ground Yourself

Sit or stand comfortably. Inhale gently, and imagine that you're gathering warmth and light inside your body. As you exhale, relax into your body and imagine that light or warmth moving down through your abdomen and into your hips, thighs, calves, and feet, and then down into the earth. Focus your attention on what it feels like to relax and let go, and if it feels right, you can make gentle spiraling movements with your arms or your body as you connect to the ground.

Grounding gives you a simple and effective way to center yourself, focus yourself, and release excess energy and tension whenever you need to.

 Write or draw what it feels like to settle into your body and focus on the present moment.

Do you have any intentional grounding practices in your daily life?

When you feel unfocused or ungrounded, how do you normally respond?

A Hands-On Grounding Practice

Another way to ground yourself is with this hands-on practice: place both of your hands on top of your head and gently run them down the sides of your head, down your neck, and down the front of your chest and abdomen. Gently bend forward as you continue running your hands down the front of your thighs and shins. When you reach your feet, imagine brushing downward into the earth.

Stand up slowly and put your hands on top of your head again and then gently run them down the sides of your head, down your neck, and down the sides of your trunk to the back of your hips. As you bend over, run your hands over your bottom and the backs of your thighs, calves, and ankles. When you reach your heels, imagine brushing downward into the earth. Repeat this process as many times as you like.

Thank the Emotions That Help You Ground and Focus Yourself

Thank your soft sadness, which helps you let go, relax, and rejuvenate yourself. And thank your soft fear, which helps you come into the present moment and maintain your calm and focused awareness.

Your Personalized Grounding Practices

What helps you center yourself when you feel ungrounded or frazzled? When you need some grounding support, you can come back here and remind yourself of things that have helped you in the past.

 Which places or activities are naturally grounding for you?

Are there people or animals who help you feel grounded?

Take a moment to list or draw a few grounding practices or activities that work well for you.

Defining Your Boundary

Having clear boundaries means knowing who you are and where you begin and end. When your boundaries are well-defined, you'll create healthy separations between your own needs, beliefs, and emotions and the needs, beliefs, and emotions of others.

Signs of boundary impairment include enmeshment, uncontrolled empathy, self-silencing, self-neglect, overbearing behavior, self-aggrandizement, addictive or compulsive behaviors, intolerance, or bullying.

Defining Your Boundary is a body-based practice that helps you build a boundary around yourself, and it relies on the ways that your brain and your nervous system already map the space around you at all times.

How to Define Your Boundary

To define your boundary, sit or stand comfortably and reach your arms straight out to either side of you (if you cannot use your arms in this way, please use your imagination).

Imagine that your fingertips are touching the edges of a lighted, oval-shaped bubble that encompasses your private, personal space. Reach your arms out in front of you and then raise them above your head. Your boundary should be an arm's length away from you at all points – in front of you, behind you, on either side of you, above you, and even underneath the floor (if that feels right to you) at that arm's length distance.

Write or draw what it feels like to be surrounded by your protective boundary.

When you can imagine this oval-shaped area all the way around you, drop your arms and let them relax. Imagine yourself surrounded by your lighted bubble at that arm's-length distance – as if you're a yolk standing inside the protective eggshell of your own imagined boundary. You may want to imagine a bright color for your boundary, which can help it feel more real to you.

Get acquainted with your personal boundary. Learn where you begin and end, and inhabit this private and defined space where you can work with your own thoughts, sensations, ideas, and emotions.

If you can imagine other people inside their own protective boundaries, you'll reinforce your own ability to maintain a healthy separation from others.

As you feel into the space around your body and imagine your healthy boundary, do you feel as if you have the right to take up this much space in the world?

    a. If not, why not?

    b. If so, where did you learn to define your healthy boundary?

Thank the Emotions That Help You Set and Maintain Your Boundary

Your boundary is sustained by your soft anger and your soft shame. When you know how to work with your anger, it will help you observe and respond to boundary challenges that may come from the exterior world. And when you know how to work with your shame (anger's friend and partner), it will help you observe and avoid boundary challenges that may come from your own actions.

Setting healthy boundaries gives you and everyone around you the space we all need to be our best selves.

 Some people set boundaries physically, with their clothing, stance, attitude, or tone of voice. Do you have any physical boundary-setting habits?

If you know someone with good interpersonal boundaries, how would you describe them?

Exploring Your Boundary

Now that you have a feel for where your boundary is, you can imagine a number of different situations and see how you and your boundary might react.

First, imagine yourself as a simple stick figure inside your healthy, arm's length boundary:

Now, breathe in gently and sigh out loud as you exhale and let go. Relax.

 Write or draw what your boundary looks like when you feel relaxed.

Now, listen for the quietest sound in your environment. You may need to relax your jaw a little or lean forward.

When you find that quietest sound, write or draw what your boundary looks like when you're aware and focused.

Now, imagine seeing someone you love very much across the room, and smile as you look toward them.

 Write or draw what your boundary looks like when you're delighted.

Now, imagine that someone at work gives you unsolicited advice.

 Write or draw what your boundary looks like when you're bothered or interrupted.

Caring for Your Boundary

As you move through your day, check in with your connection to your boundaries. Your boundaries are a part of your nervous system and your sense of where you are in time and space. Your boundaries are a part of you, and they respond to the things you experience.

If you find that you're very sensitive and likely to lose your sense of boundaries in certain situations, you can write or draw what you're sensing. When you know what's happening, you can imagine strengthening your boundaries – making them thicker or brighter, or imagining a sound where your boundary meets the outside world.

You can also use clothing and space as a boundary; for instance, you can wear a scarf, tie, hat, or jewelry to set a boundary, or you can arrange your home or workspace to create some breathing space when you need it.

Make a list of the physical boundaries you rely on in your everyday life.

You have a right to healthy boundaries, and noticing how your boundary responds (and how the people you admire set boundaries) can help you understand the specific kinds of boundary support you need.

Your Personalized Boundary Practices

What helps you set and maintain your boundary? What helps you when your sense of your own boundaries is not strong? Your personalized practices will be here as a reminder when you need support!

 Take a moment to list or draw any practices or activities that help you regain your sense of your own supportive personal space.

Conscious Complaining

Being able to complain consciously gives a voice to your struggles, which restores your flow, your energy, and your hope. This solo emotional channeling practice helps you access your emotions and discover the truth of what's going on when you're feeling moody.

Situations that Conscious Complaining can address include difficult problems, relationship troubles, *unconscious* complaining, self-silencing, repetitive worry, apathy, anger, depression, confusion, shame, despair, or any other trapped emotions.

 What is your current attitude about complaining?

Do you normally take the time you need to complain about difficult things? If not, why not?

How to Complain Consciously

Find a private, solitary place where you can really whine and gripe (or cry) about the frustration, hopelessness, or absurdity of your situation. Start your complaining with some sort of phrase, such as "I'm complaining now!" You can also grab some paper and write down your complaints if that works better for you.

If you're inside, you can complain to the walls or furniture, to a mirror, or to whatever strikes your fancy. If you're outside, you can complain to plants and trees, animals, nature, the sky, or your god or guiding spirits.

If you're a strong complainer, you might want to create a complaining shrine for yourself (maybe on top of a dresser or an out-of-the-way table), with supportive pictures of grumpy cats, bratty kids, barking dogs, political cartoons, and whatever else calls to your complaining nature.

Remember that your vocabulary has power, so use the Emotional Vocabulary List on pages 161-166 to find words for the specific intensity levels of each emotion you feel. This will help you develop a stronger emotional vocabulary, which will help you develop stronger emotion regulation skills.

 You can list some key vocabulary words that describe how you're feeling when you're complaining here:

Complain for as long as you like (you'll be surprised at how quickly this works), then thank whatever you've been whining or griping at, and end your Conscious Complaining session by bowing, shaking off, and then doing something you really like to do.

When you have full permission to complain within this private ceremonial framework, you'll find that your emotions will help you identify your problems. Then, it will be much easier to understand and address those problems because the gifts and skills in your emotions will be available to you.

Thank the Emotions That Conscious Complaining Helps You Access

Conscious Complaining is an emotional channeling practice that helps you access *all* of your emotions. Most of us are taught to repress or ignore our emotions, and that creates a backlog of unfelt, unheard, and unaddressed emotions. This practice helps you become aware of what your emotions are trying to tell you.

This may sound contradictory, but you just can't be happy – and you can't access the gifts in all of your emotions – unless you complain (consciously) when you truly need to.

Your Personalized Conscious Complaining Practice

When we're filled with frustration or despair or biting complaints about the unfairness of life, many of us have no practices at all to support ourselves, and we suffer needlessly. This Conscious Complaining practice helps you access your healing awareness and emotional skills when you truly need them!

 Take a moment to list a few difficult situations in your life that could benefit from Conscious Complaining.

Now choose one of these situations and observe what happens when you complain consciously about it (either verbally or in writing), and jot down your impressions here.

Conscious Complaining with a Partner

Being able to complain with willing partners can give you an excellent way to de-steam without blowing up, and it helps strengthen and nurture your relationships.

Situations that Conscious Complaining with a Partner can address include relationship troubles, difficult problems, and repetitive or trapped emotions.

How to Consciously Complain with a Partner

In this partner practice, one person listens supportively for three minutes while the other person complains, and then the partners switch places. Note that it's important that the partners trust each other and that there's not a power imbalance in the relationship.

 Who would you want to share this practice with?

Another very important rule is that you can't complain about your *listener* because that wouldn't be fair. If someone is willing to listen and provide support for your complaining, then complaining about them would be like taking a hostage! This practice is for times when the problems you're complaining about are *outside* of your relationship.

If you're the complainer, you start by acknowledging that the complaining needs to happen. You could say, "I don't need you to fix me. I just need to complain," or "I need to complain consciously; do you have some time for a trade?"

Then you can bring up whatever is stuck in your craw: "Things are just rotten, this situation is bothering me, things are too hard," etc. Set a timer for three minutes and complain until your time is up.

Your listener's job is to support your complaining with supportive "uh-huhs" and gestures – no advice, no suggestions, just support. Your listener creates a safe haven for your complaining, which immediately makes your complaining feel less toxic.

When your turn is over, close in a clear way, such as saying, "Thanks, that's been bugging me," or "I'm done, thanks!"

Then, you trade positions: your listener now gets to do three minutes of Conscious Complaining while you listen and provide support (but no advice!). When both of you are done, this practice is complete.

 What was it like to be allowed to complain out loud without your partner offering advice or trying to change the way you think and feel?

What was it like for you to listen to your partner's complaints and know that you didn't have to solve anything?

You may be surprised by how productive (and funny) this partner complaining practice is. We're all taught to be endlessly positive and peppy, which means that we have to repress most of our emotions. Sadly, this repression tends to clog us up with all of the things we're not allowed to say or notice or feel. This partner practice helps you restore your emotional flow, and it clears you out and brings back your perspective and your sense of humor. And because you're not expected to solve anything for each other, this practice won't add problems to your already difficult situations.

There's also an extra benefit for both of you: instead of isolating yourselves, you can learn how to reach out when you're in turmoil in a safe, honest, empathy-building, and emotionally intelligent way.

Your Personalized Conscious Complaining with a Partner Practices

Many of us isolate ourselves when we face difficult or ongoing problems, or we complain *unconsciously*, which can burden others. In the space below, write down a few difficult situations you've faced recently, and think about people you could share this practice with. If you've tended to be an unconscious complainer, your people would most likely appreciate learning and sharing this practice with you!

The Troubling Situation	My Ideal Conscious Complaining Partner

Ethical Empathic Gossip

Gossip is usually seen as a terrible thing, but anthropologists and social scientists see gossip as the tool we use to share and understand informal or unwritten social and emotional rules. Gossip is a vital part of social life, communication, and emotional health, and studies have shown that gossip is universal and is used by people of all ages and genders.

Gossip is also a special tool for what I call the "sociological emotions" – namely, jealousy and envy, each of which gathers astonishing amounts of information about our relationships and our social world. However, a massive problem with gossip is that it can train us to talk *about* people, rather than talking *to* them. Gossip can also lead us to invade the privacy of the people we gossip about as we broadcast their behavior all over the place.

If we can understand the powerful social and emotional information gossip provides, we can turn gossip into an intentional communication practice that supports our emotions, our ethics, our healthy empathy, and our relationships. We can turn gossip into an *ethical empathic practice*.

The practice of Ethical Empathic Gossip will connect you to the deep, essential, and emotionally rich undercurrents that exist in gossip and in your informal gossip networks. Any stuck relationship, emotion, or situation can be addressed with Ethical Empathic Gossip, and as you learn to gossip ethically with your chosen partners, you'll become more informed and empathic about yourself and others, more skilled and emotionally agile in your relationships, and more comfortable in your social world. Gossip is a truly brilliant communication tool – as long as it's *ethical and empathic* gossip.

 What trusted person would you want as your Ethical Empathic Gossip partner? (Make sure you feel safe with this person and that there isn't a power imbalance between you!)

Here are the guidelines for Ethical Empathic Gossip with a supportive partner (each turn generally takes about thirteen minutes):

1. Identify a person you gossip about consistently, and with whom your relationship has stalled.

2. Open the gossip session by acknowledging your trouble in the relationship.

3. Ask your partner for help in dealing with your troubled relationship. Ask for opinions, ideas, techniques, and skills that will help you reenter the relationship in a different way.

4. Go for it – just gossip.

5. When your partner gives you feedback, pay attention.

6. Close the gossip session by thanking your partner and then go back to the damaged relationship with your new skills and insights, or modify the relationship if it's too damaged to survive as is. Don't go back in the same old way, because that's what led to the need for unempathic or unethical gossip in the first place.

When you're done, you can trade places with your partner if they would like to take a turn. Although these turns ideally take about thirteen minutes, they can go as long as twenty minutes per person when people know each other well. Set a timer, but don't cut people off if they're on a roll; jealousy and envy hold so much information that they may need time to sort out all of the complexities.

 Now, think about situations in which you tend to gossip about others rather than speak with them directly:

What kinds of support are you seeking from your gossip partner(s)?

What kinds of information are you sharing?

What prevents you from speaking directly to the person in question?

Now think about situations in which someone gossips to you:

What kinds of support are they seeking from you?

What kinds of information are they sharing?

Why are they unable to speak directly to the person in question?

Thank the Emotions That Ethical Empathic Gossip Helps You Access

The sociological emotions of jealousy and envy keep careful tabs on every part of your life and all of your relationships. This practice can help you access their wisdom and gain deep understanding of yourself and others.

When your gossip is conscious and ethical, you'll increase your social skills and your empathy, and you'll become more able to create honest and healthy relationships. Learning to gossip ethically will also remind you that you can always ask for – and receive – help in dealing with difficult emotions and difficult people.

Your Personalized Ethical Empathic Gossip Practices

In the space below, write down people you've gossiped about (or wanted to gossip about) and what your jealousy and envy were telling you about them.

The Person I Gossip About	What Unmet Desires or Inequalities Are Present?

Burning Contracts

Burning Contracts is an emotional channeling practice that helps you identify unconscious agreements and behaviors so that you can release them consciously.

Situations that Burning Contracts can address include unworkable relationships, repetitive thoughts, unresolved emotions, hopelessness, trapped feelings, and/or unwanted habits and behaviors.

Each of us relies on many agreed upon (or enforced) contractual behaviors that help us make our way through life. We *learn* how to behave in different contexts, situations, and relationships, though this learning is often unconsciously done. We enter into these behaviors and contracts for important reasons, but we always have the right to end them if they no longer work for us. Most importantly, we can then learn new ways to behave and respond that work better for who we are now.

 What kinds of unhealthy contracts have you agreed to without thinking?

What do you think would have happened if you hadn't agreed?

What kinds of healthy contracts do you have in your life right now?

What is the difference between situations that lead you to agree to healthy contracts and situations that lead you to agree to unhealthy ones?

How to Burn a Contract

Imagine unrolling a large, blank piece of paper in front of you (inside your boundary). Some people imagine that this contract is flat on a table, while others imagine it in front of them, as if it's a whiteboard or a movie screen. Others like this contract to have depth, as if it's a basket that can hold anything you put into it. You can also write your contract on an actual piece of paper if that works best for you.

 Think about or write on a separate sheet of paper about something that has been bothering you, such as an ongoing problem that just won't shift. The situation and your responses to it are important parts of your contract. You can project, write, speak, or think your problem onto your real or imagined contract.

Here are some examples of what you might place in your contract:

Emotional expectations: How you're supposed to feel and express yourself

Intellectual rules: How and what you're supposed to think; what intelligence looks like

Physical rules: How your body is supposed to look and perform for others

Spiritual expectations: How you're supposed to meditate, pray, or behave

Entire relationships: Images of yourself, your partner(s), and the ways you interact

When you've filled your contract with words, images, emotions, or thoughts, you'll close it in some way. This important step helps you bring a physical sense of finality to this unworkable contract. If your contract is on paper, roll it up tightly so the material inside can no longer be seen, and destroy it (crumple it, burn it, or trash it). If your contract is in your imagination, visualize rolling it up, tossing it away from you, and burning it with whatever emotional energy you feel.

Repeat this process with a new contract or a fresh piece of paper until you feel a shift of some kind. Then this contract-burning session will be done!

When you can clearly identify your contracts – these unwanted behaviors, ideas, or relationships – you can begin to separate yourself from them. In this mindful space, you can see yourself not as a victim of these behaviors or situations, but as an upright person who *decided* to act, relate, and behave in these ways, and who can now decide to act, relate, and behave differently.

Thank the Emotions That Burning Contracts Helps You Access

Welcome your emotions – whatever they are. They'll provide the energy you need to identify your contracts, destroy them, and set yourself free. Your emotions are always paying attention to you, and they'll definitely perk up when you begin to identify things that simply don't work for you. You can use whichever emotions arise to move these ideas and behaviors out of unconscious habit and into your conscious awareness.

For instance, if you feel angry, you can set a boundary between yourself and your contract and make a strong and clear separation from it. If you feel anxious, you can speed up what you're doing and lean into the motivational energy anxiety brings to you. If you're feeling grief or sadness, you can slow down and really feel into the loss and the letting go. And so forth.

Your emotions help you feel into what's important for you, and you can rely on their wisdom and energy to help you make healing changes in your life.

Your Personalized Burning Contracts Practices

 Take a moment to write down or draw some contractual behaviors and expectations that don't work for you and see if you can dislodge them with Burning Contracts. If you have a hard time with the idea of completely destroying your contracts (because you don't know what could replace them), see the Renegotiating Contracts practice on the next page.

Renegotiating Contracts

When you use the Burning Contracts practice, you can free yourself from ideas that were guiding your thoughts, emotions, behaviors, and actions in ways that no longer work for you. Burning Contracts can help you become aware of the rules, expectations, and shoulds that you've outgrown. Becoming aware of and then burning your outdated contracts can set you free.

You can also build more freedom for yourself by creating new and intentional contracts that are meaningful and workable for you now. Some contracts that are harmful need to be destroyed completely, but some may contain important ethics and values, even though the contract itself creates problems. These are contracts that you can *renegotiate*.

How to Renegotiate a Contract

To renegotiate an outdated or troubling contract, follow these steps:

 Get two pieces of blank paper and at the top of the first one write, "Aspects of the Unworkable Contract." At the top of the second piece of paper write, "What I Would Prefer." On the first piece of paper, make a list of eight to twelve rules or behaviors that the old, unworkable contract requires of you. It may help to use bullet points.

When you've got a good sense of this unworkable contract, ground yourself and define your boundaries. Feel into the emotional tone and expectations of the unworkable contract on the first piece of paper, and on the second piece, create a corresponding list of bullet points for things that you would prefer and that would help you feel grounded and well-defined.

Here are some simple examples of how this renegotiation process might look:

Aspects of the Unworkable Contract	What I Would Prefer
Big boys don't cry.	Boys and men can cry whenever they want.
Being empathic means never saying no.	Healthy empathy requires healthy boundaries.
The needs of others always come first.	I will help when I can, but self-care is a must.

When you're happy with your renegotiated contract, put it in a place of honor where you can refer to it regularly. You could post it on your refrigerator or your wall, make a beautiful altar for it, or carry it with you wherever you go.

 Which emotion(s) do you feel when you realize that you need to renegotiate a contract?

How does your boundary look and feel in the presence of an old, outdated contract?

How does your boundary look and feel when you renegotiate an old contract and create a better one?

Thank the Emotions That Help You Renegotiate Your Contracts

This practice relies on the gifts of many emotions; for instance, sadness will help you ground yourself and let go of things that aren't working any longer; anger will help you define your boundaries and identify what you value; fear will help you focus yourself and identify what's changing; shame will help you uphold healthy new behaviors; envy will help you identify what you desire; contentment will let you know when you've done good work; and so forth.

You can invite your emotions to help you negotiate the best contracts for your present-day needs.

Your Personalized Renegotiating Contracts Practice

Many of us never learned how to renegotiate the behaviors and expectations we've agreed to. It is as if they are written in stone. This renegotiation practice can help you reclaim your autonomy and bring healing flexibility to all parts of your life.

 Take a moment to write down or draw situations and relationships that have become stuck or that won't let you grow as a person. Know that you can make changes and declare what you'd prefer – even if the situations or behaviors have very deep roots. Your emotions will help you identify these problem areas, and then they'll help you address them!

Rejuvenation

Rejuvenation is a healing practice that recruits many of your emotions to help you relax, restore yourself, and embody sacred space.

Situations that Rejuvenation can address include overwhelm, tension, world-weariness, fatigue, illness, loss, overwork, or any other situation where you lose your inner connection to pleasure and joy.

How to Rejuvenate Yourself

To begin, imagine your personal boundary as strong, whole, and vibrant. In the space between your body and the edge of your boundary, imagine your favorite place in the world at your favorite time of day.

For instance, feel yourself surrounded by a mountainside on a late spring evening, beside a creek in a redwood grove at dawn, or on a tropical beach at the perfect time of day. Surround yourself with this feeling of beauty, relaxation, and delicious, sensual pleasure. Let your focus drift naturally and embody the way you feel when you're in your favorite place.

As you sense your favorite nature scene around you, breathe some of these delicious, peaceful feelings into your body. Take a gentle breath and imagine breathing the felt sense of this serene and beautiful place into your head and neck. Breathe this feeling down into your chest, your arms, and your hands. Breathe it in through your chest and abdomen and into your lower belly, then exhale it down into your legs and feet. Breathe this delightful feeling into every part of your body. Fill yourself with this sense of utter relaxation and beauty.

When you feel full, let your body, your emotions, and your focus soften and relax. You can stay here for as long as you like, but to complete this Rejuvenation practice, bend over and touch the floor with your hands, and let your head hang down (if you can't use your body in this way, please use your imagination). Just relax. If you're in public and you can't touch the floor, you can take a gentle breath and ground yourself. You're done!

You can surround yourself with this healing scene whenever you like. Rejuvenation is a completely portable emotional healing practice.

Our busy lives tend to give us no time for rest or rejuvenation. Have you been able to carve out restful time for yourself, and if so, how have you done that?

What gets in the way of your rest and rejuvenation practices, if anything?

Thank the Emotions That Help You Rejuvenate Yourself

Rejuvenation helps you access soft joy, which arises to help you feel a blissful sense of expansiveness and connection to beauty, pleasure, and wonder. Rejuvenation also recruits the gifts of happiness and contentment as it fills you with delicious sensations, and it recruits the healing gifts of jealousy and envy as you identify the most wonderful places, the most wonderful surroundings, and the most wonderful sensations. What's more, this practice recruits the gifts of sadness and grief as you relax, let go, and allow the things you don't need to fall away, and truly release those things that have ended.

Your Personalized Rejuvenation Practices

What rejuvenates you? Each of us has different things that delight and replenish us.

 Take a moment to jot down or draw the things that refresh and delight you and come back here for a reminder when you need a rejuvenating break.

PART 3

The Seventeen Emotions

All of your emotions contain specific gifts, skills, and intelligence, and learning their language can help you become more aware of your inner and outer life and understand yourself and others more deeply.

In this section, you'll find detailed descriptions of each of your emotions, including the gifts and skills they bring to you, vocabulary words to help you identify them, questions that help you work directly with them, and practices to access the healing wisdom they contain.

THE ANGER FAMILY
Boundaries, Rules, and Behavioral Guidelines

Anger ~ Apathy ~ Shame/Guilt ~ Hatred

The emotions in the anger family tell you when a boundary has
been crossed or a rule has been broken. They help you create
values-based behavioral guidelines for yourself and others.

Anger: The Honorable Sentry

The Gifts and Skills in Anger	Honor ~ Self-awareness ~ Healthy self-esteem Proper boundaries ~ Healthy detachment Protection of yourself and others
The Internal Questions for Anger	*What do I value?* *What must be protected and restored?*
Some Nuances of Anger	**Soft Anger**: Annoyed, Determined, Frustrated, Protective **Medium Anger**: Angry, Courageous, Mad, Offended **Intense Anger**: Furious, Incensed, Livid, Righteous

ANGER arises when there are challenges to what you value, your self-image, your behaviors, or your interpersonal boundaries – or when you see these things being challenged in someone else. Anger arises in the presence of something that's valuable to you, because you don't get angry about something that has no meaning. Therefore, anger can help you understand exactly who you are and what you want and need – as an individual and as a member of social groups. Your anger gives you a strong sense of self-confidence and the ability to support self-confidence in others as well.

Anger's job is to help you set and maintain healthy boundaries around what you value. When it's soft and free-flowing, your anger helps you uphold mutual respect and keep open the lines of communication in your relationships.

However, most of us were not taught to recognize our emotions at their softer levels, so we tend to identify anger only after it gets to the level of an intense mood. Many people don't know how to work with intense anger, so they may repress it and lose their boundaries, or they may explode with their anger and offend against the boundaries of others.

How were you taught to work with anger when you were little?

How did your family work with anger?

Have you ever seen someone work with anger in a healthy and respectful way?

Anger is a wonderful and respectful emotion when you know how to work with it; it can help you stay true to yourself and remain honorable in your interactions with others. Anger brings you energy, intensity, and certainty – and asking its internal questions (*What do I value?* and *What must be protected and restored?*) – will help you maintain your boundaries and your convictions as you channel your anger into healthy and honorable words and deeds.

 What is one situation that reliably engages your anger?

a. How are your boundaries challenged in this situation?

b. How do you reset your boundaries in this situation?

Some Notes about Anger

A key to working skillfully with your anger is to become aware of it at its soft level, *before* it escalates to an intensity that you might not be able to manage. Explore the soft anger words in the Emotional Vocabulary List on page 161 and practice responding to your anger when it's subtle. This will help you develop awareness and skills for times when your anger needs to arise in its more intense forms.

Practices to Help You Work with Your Anger

Empathic Mindfulness Practices: Grounding and Focusing ~ Hands-On Grounding ~ Defining Your Boundary ~ Burning Contracts ~ Conscious Complaining (solo and with a partner) ~ Rejuvenation ~ Ethical Empathic Gossip

Additional Practices: Setting clear and loving boundaries ~ Identifying your values (see the next section)

It may be useful to circle the practices above that feel supportive to you or that would have helped the last time you felt quite angry.

Personalizing Your Anger Practices

Take a moment to feel into the anger questions: **What do I value? What must be protected and restored?**

Identifying what you value is an essential part of individuation. The things you find valuable define you and set your boundaries, just as anger does. Knowing what's important to you helps you understand what needs to be protected and restored.

 Take a moment to write down ten (or more) things that you value (such as honesty, your relationships, empathy, humor, etc.).

Apathy (or Boredom): The Protective Mask for Anger

The Gifts and Skills in Apathy	Detachment ~ Boundary setting ~ Separation Taking a pause
The Internal Questions for Apathy	*What is being avoided?* *What can be made conscious?*
Some Nuances of Apathy	**Soft Apathy**: Ambivalent, Detached, Disengaged, Uninspired **Medium Apathy:** Apathetic, Bored, Indifferent, Protected **Intense Apathy:** Bored stiff, Numb, Shielded, Tuned out

APATHY (or boredom) arises in places where your needs and values are unimportant, or in situations where there isn't room for who you are. Apathy can provide you with a type of protective boundary when you either cannot or will not set boundaries or express your needs and values openly.

Apathy is a protective mask for anger. It can give you an excellent time-out when you need to disengage – such as when your needs are not important, or when you're in a place where clear anger would be out of place or would expose you to unwanted attention.

In this masking state, you can protect yourself with an attitude that can create distance and a sense of having some control over the situation. The "I don't care, I can't be bothered, whatever" behavior of apathy is a way to set boundaries, even in situations where your boundaries and your needs are unimportant and unwelcome.

The masking state of apathy is necessary and helpful, but it's important to be aware of it so that it doesn't take you completely out of commission.

Apathy helps you take a break when you're unable or unwilling to speak up or set a boundary. What situations normally bring your apathy forward?

What do you usually do when you feel bored or apathetic?

Your apathy can help you take small vacations from focus and hard work – and you'll be able to daydream, detach, or plop yourself in front of the computer or a book when you need a break. When you're ready to refocus, you can ask yourself the questions for apathy (*What is being avoided?* and *What can be made conscious?*) and uncover the anger or other emotions that are being masked and protected.

What supports you when you're in boring or unwelcoming situations?

Some Notes about Apathy

There is almost no room for us to be bored or apathetic, even though apathy has a vital role in keeping us whole in tedious and unwelcoming situations. You may have heard that boredom is a sign of your lack of imagination, or proof that you need to pay better attention or work harder, but neither of these insults are true (or helpful). I call apathy a masking state for a reason!

Practices to Help You Work with Your Apathy

Empathic Mindfulness Practices: Grounding and Focusing ~ Defining Your Boundary ~ Burning Contracts ~ Conscious Complaining (solo and with a partner) ~ Rejuvenation ~ Ethical Empathic Gossip

Additional Practices: Taking a break ~ Detaching intentionally ~ Letting yourself daydream

It may be useful to circle the practices above that help when you feel apathetic.

Personalizing Your Apathy Practices

Take a moment to feel into the apathy questions: *What is being avoided? What can be made conscious?*

Apathy is not a failure on your part. It's perfectly fine to be bored and apathetic and to take a break when you need one. It's fine to ignore boundary-challenging situations if you just don't have the energy, or if speaking up would accomplish nothing (or backfire). However, you can bring consciousness to your apathy and use the downtime it provides to think of (or dream of) situations or relationships where your needs, your voice, and your boundaries *are* welcomed and respected.

The next time you're bored, ask yourself, "What would be interesting and welcoming for me?" Even in tedious environments that have no room for you or your needs, this simple question can help you access your imagination, your intentions, and your own sense of how you want the world to be.

Think about a regularly boring situation where your apathy is necessary and write down a few interesting and welcoming things you would prefer.

The Boring Situation	What I Would Prefer

Shame and Guilt: Restoring Integrity

The Gifts and Skills in Shame	Atonement ~ Integrity ~ Conscience Self-respect ~ Behavioral change
The Internal Questions for Shame	*Whose ethics and values have been disrespected? What must be made right?*
Some Nuances of Shame	**Soft Shame:** Conscientious, Ethical, Hesitant, Restrained **Medium Shame:** Ashamed, Moral, Regretful, Sorry **Intense Shame:** Disgraced, Humiliated, Incorruptible, Mortified

SHAME arises when you've done something (or are about to do something) that disrespects your boundaries or the boundaries of others. I separate shame from guilt because shame is an emotion, while guilt is a statement of fact. You're either guilty or not guilty – and when you are guilty, the emotion you should feel is *shame*.

Instead of trying to erase shame, we focus on the messages and contracts your shame is trying to uphold. When these messages are authentic and appropriate, they come from your own moral code and from rules and ethics that are supportive for you. These messages can feel like your moral structure, and when you step away from them, your shame usually arises in a way you can work with.

But when these messages are inauthentic or inappropriate, they usually come from outside sources (such as authorities or the media) who want to control you. When you try to step away from these inappropriate or controlling shaming messages, you may feel deep pain and a sense of being trapped.

Most of us learn about shame by **being** shamed. As you think of two things that you feel ashamed about, can you track these shaming messages to their source?

    a. Who shamed you about these things?

    b. Who does this shame belong to?

Write or draw what your boundary looks like in the presence of these two shaming messages.

Burning Contracts (see pages 55-58) helps you put an end to painful or inappropriate shaming contracts so that you and your shame can focus on ethics and values that nourish you. When you can work well with your own authentic and appropriate shaming messages, you'll stop yourself *before* you do something hurtful, *before* you say the wrong thing, or *before* you enter into unhealthy behaviors or relationships.

Interestingly, when your shame is working gracefully, you won't feel it as shame. Instead, you'll just behave in a way that makes you feel comfortable and proud of yourself. Shame is an essential social emotion, and when it's based on healing and appropriate shaming messages, you may not even feel it.

If you don't know why your shame has come forward, you can ask the internal questions and apologize or make amends if necessary: *Whose ethics and values have been disrespected? What must be made right?* Once you act to correct your wrongdoing, your shame will recede naturally.

Your shame will help you turn away from harmful or self-absorbed impulses – even when no one is looking. It will keep you punctual, polite, and kind, and it will lead you gently but firmly away from trouble and turmoil. With the honorable assistance of your shame, you'll experience healthy and appropriate integrity and self-respect.

 Healthy shaming messages don't usually feel painful; they feel like a sense of accomplishment, dedication, and respectful self-discipline. Write down a behavior you're proud of:

a. How did you learn this behavior?

b. How do you maintain it?

c. Where does your dedication come from?

Write or draw what your boundary looks like when you feel accomplished, respectful, and proud of yourself.

Some Notes about Shame

If your shame feels miserable and will not calm down even after you make amends and change your behavior, you are very likely dealing with inauthentic shaming messages. The Burning Contracts practices (see pages 55-58) can help you identify where you picked up these unwelcome visitors so that you can separate yourself from their unhealthy influence.

Practices to Help You Work with Your Shame

Empathic Mindfulness Practices: Grounding and Focusing ~ Hands-On Grounding ~ Defining Your Boundary ~ Burning Contracts ~ Renegotiating Contracts ~ Rejuvenation ~ Ethical Empathic Gossip

Additional Practices: Listening to your conscience ~ Identifying your workable and unworkable shaming messages ~ Observing your behaviors with integrity Making amends

It may be useful to circle the practices above that would help when you feel ashamed.

Personalizing Your Shame Practices

Take a moment to feel into the shame questions: *Whose ethics and values have been disrespected? What must be made right?*

Sometimes, it's *your* ethics and values that are being disrespected – *by you!* When you disrespect your own ethics and values, how do you feel, and how do you make things right? And when you realize that you've disrespected the ethics and values of others, how do you feel, and how do you make amends?

 Take a moment to write down a few situations where you successfully apologized and made amends (to yourself and others).

What I Did	How I Felt	How I Made Things Right

Hatred: The Profound Mirror

The Gifts and Skills in Hatred	Intense awareness ~ Piercing vision ~ Sudden evolution ~ Shadow Work
The Internal Questions for Hatred	*What has fallen into my shadow?* *What must be reintegrated?*
Some Nuances of Hatred	**Soft Hatred:** Annoyed, Aware of your shadow, Bristling, Irritated **Medium Hatred:** Antagonized, Hateful, Resentful, Self-aware **Intense Hatred:** Contemptuous, Loathing, Righteous, Shadow resourced

HATRED arises in the presence of your *shadow*, or those things that you cannot accept in yourself or despise in others. If you know how to work with it, hatred can help you hold up a mirror to the unwanted and unacknowledged parts of yourself.

Hatred is not mere dislike, which goes away when you separate yourself from people who behave badly, and it isn't fear, which fades when you get away from scary situations. Hatred is an intense flare of disgust and anger, which means you're dealing with severe boundary problems and the near-complete loss of your integrity and balance.

When hatred arises, you're in some ways reacting to things you see in your hate target, but you're also shining a rage-powered spotlight on serious boundary issues in the shadows of your own soul.

When we express hatred, we fool ourselves into thinking that we're totally separate from our hate targets – that we're nothing like them or that we're stronger, truer, and better than they are. If this were true, though, we'd have appropriate boundaries and the ability to treat these people with respect. But we don't. When we express hatred at others, we lose our honor and even our conscience.

When hatred arises, it's a message from deep inside yourself: *Here are the things I can't embody yet. Here is where I have utterly lost my way.* If you can learn to catch yourself before you act on your hatred, you can use its power to learn vital things about yourself and make powerful changes in your life.

In fact, it's possible that many deep and buried issues cannot be fully experienced until the fierce emotion of hatred arises, because without its power and intensity, you might not be able to make the great leap from business-as-usual into the searing and necessary self-awareness that hatred can bring to you.

A Simple Practice to Identify Hatred: Me, Not Me, and the Other

A simple way to enter into the territory of your own shadow is to list qualities that describe you (Me) and those that don't (Not Me). In the first two rows of the table below are two examples of my own Me and Not Me attributes.

 Add some of your own personal Me qualities in the left column and your Not Me qualities in the right column in the extra rows below.

Me	Not Me
College educated	Uneducated
Disabled	Able-bodied

These Me and Not Me categories may include some shadowy aspects for you, but because we started out with simple qualities, it's not likely that you'll feel a lot of hatred. However, if you add the category of The Other (or that which you would *never* choose to be), you may discover a shadow lurking.

You may find that these Other people raise your hackles – perhaps subtly or perhaps intensely. Something about them will draw your eye, and you may become somewhat hyperfocused on them. One of the reasons that hatred can destabilize your boundaries is that you may actually project your own assumptions, emotions, and unmet needs onto your Other.

When you find your Other, you are in the territory of the shadow. When you're hyperfocused on your Other and projecting a great deal, you'll actually break your own boundaries from the inside out, and you'll essentially enter into an enmeshed relationship with your Other. This is why hatred is so powerful. It's alerting you to an unhealthy level of boundary loss and enmeshment.

List the qualities of one or two of your Other people below my examples in the following table.

Me	Not Me	The Other
College educated	Uneducated	People who got PhDs they didn't deserve
Disabled	Able-bodied	People who treat disabled folks as incompetent

Generally, these qualities are ones that have been denied to you, and you may either react strongly to them or refuse to allow them in yourself, sometimes to your detriment. For instance, you may write down *selfish* or *privileged*, and it can be illuminating to wonder if you ever allow yourself to focus entirely on yourself, or if you allow yourself to celebrate your own place of privilege (earned or not). The qualities you despise in others can often show you important things about how you've learned to treat yourself.

Some Notes about Hatred and Shadow Work

Shadow Work is a practice that helps you uncover and work with your hatred so that it won't endanger you or others. Shadow Work helps you face and reintegrate the lost parts of yourself so that you can evolve and become whole. There are many excellent books about Shadow Work in the Resources section at the end of this workbook.

Practices to Help You Work with Your Hatred

Empathic Mindfulness Practices: Grounding and Focusing ~ Defining Your Boundary ~ Burning Contracts ~ Renegotiating Contracts ~ Conscious Complaining (solo and with a partner) ~ Ethical Empathic Gossip ~ Rejuvenation

Additional Practices: The Me, Not Me, and The Other ~ Shadow Work ~ Bringing a sense of humor to your shadow

It may be useful to circle the practices above that help you do your Shadow Work and reintegrate yourself.

Personalizing Your Hatred Practices

Take a moment to feel into the hatred questions: *What has fallen into my shadow? What must be reintegrated?*

The Me, Not Me, and The Other practice can help you take a quick inventory of anyone or any group that is moving into the othered shadow for you. But it can also help to come up with a general list of the qualities you cannot tolerate in others (sort of an *anti*-things-I-value list, in contrast to the values list you made in the anger section).

These qualities, such as *selfishness* or *meanness*, may be universal dislikes, but they may also hold some personal shadow for you and give you opportunities for Shadow Work and shadow integration (if you wish).

 Take a moment to list some of the qualities you cannot tolerate (and your reactions to them), and feel into whether they need to be integrated.

Unwanted Qualities	My Emotional Responses	Does This Need Integration?

THE FEAR FAMILY

Instincts, Intuition, and Orienting

Fear ~ Anxiety ~ Confusion ~ Jealousy ~ Envy ~ Panic

The emotions in the fear family contain your intuition and your
instincts. They help you orient yourself to your surroundings,
notice change, novelty, or hazards, and take effective action.

Fear: Instincts, Intuition, and Action

The Gifts and Skills in Fear	Curiosity ~ Intuition ~ Instincts ~ Focus Clarity ~ Attentiveness ~ Readiness ~ Vigor
The Internal Questions for Fear	*What am I sensing?* *What action should be taken?*
Some Nuances of Fear	**Soft Fear**: Alert, Instinctive, Intuitive, Watchful **Medium Fear**: Afraid, Focused, Unsettled, Vigorous **Intense Fear**: Frenzied, Hyperactivated, Laser focused, Petrified

FEAR helps you focus on the present moment, access your instincts, and tune into changes in your environment. Most people have been taught to see fear as the enemy, and even the mention of the word *fear* can make them uncomfortable. If you think of the ways we talk about fear, you may have a hard time recalling anything that suggests that fear might be a useful or necessary emotion. People usually treat fear as toxic and unwanted: "There's no need to be afraid," "There's nothing to fear but fear itself," or this simple slogan that was made into a bumper sticker: "No fear!"

Here's the problem: Fear is an essential emotion that brings you clarity, instincts, and intuition. Fear helps you stay focused and ready to respond to your environment. If you come upon something startling or dangerous, your awareness and readiness will allow you to act in ways that protect you and the people around you. Without your fear, you're not a superhero. Without your fear, you're unaware and unprotected.

You don't need to feel obviously afraid to access the gifts of fear. Here's an example of soft, free-flowing fear: Think about your behavior when you drive your car skillfully. You check your mirrors, watch traffic, maneuver your car, and avoid hazards. All of these actions require being in the present moment – focused and aware – and being connected to your healthy instincts and your fear.

If you're capable, aware, intuitive, and focused, you're already connected to your soft fear. All you need to do now is identify your fear correctly, welcome it, and thank it for all its help. Fear is not your enemy. In fact, it may be one of the most essential friends you have.

 Think about situations where you have felt calm, intuitive, graceful, and grounded. What was it about these situations that kept your fear soft and free-flowing?

Write or draw what your boundary felt like during these softer activations of fear.

Now think about situations where you have felt restless, suspicious, and ungrounded. What was it about these situations that kept your fear more activated?

Write or draw what your boundary felt like when your fear needed to be at a medium or intense level of activation.

Some Notes about Fear

Fear brings you the awareness, instincts, and intuition you need to monitor your environment and keep yourself alert and aware – and fear is focused in the present moment. If something is looming in the future, then *anxiety* will arise to help you plan and prepare. And if something is truly hazardous to you, then *panic* will arise to help you protect yourself with your fight, flee, freeze, or flock-to-safety instincts.

Practices to Help You Work with Your Fear

Empathic Mindfulness Practices: Grounding and Focusing ~ Hands-On Grounding ~ Defining Your Boundary ~ Rejuvenation

Additional Practices: Listening to yourself ~ Checking in with your body ~ Staying curious

It may be useful to circle the practices above that feel supportive when your fear needs your attention.

Personalizing Your Fear Practices

Take a moment to feel into the fear questions: *What am I sensing? What action should be taken?*

Most of us have been taught to push through our fear or treat it as an unwanted visitor. This unhealthy training separates us from our instincts and our intuition, but luckily we can reclaim our good sense when we can connect with our fear.

 Write down a few statements, gestures, or bodily postures that would help you slow down and listen when your fear needs you to focus on the present moment. For instance, you could raise your hand gently and say, "Hold on; I'm sensing something." Or you could breathe and center yourself so that you can home in on your instincts and your intuition.

My Fear-Supporting Actions

Anxiety: Focus, Motivation, and Completion

The Gifts and Skills in Anxiety	Motivation ~ Foresight ~ Focus Preparation ~ Task completion Procrastination support system
The Internal Questions for Anxiety	*What brought this feeling forward?* *What **truly** needs to be done?*
Some Nuances of Anxiety	**Soft Anxiety:** Capable, Clear-headed, Organized, Prepared **Medium Anxiety**: Activated, Anxious, Forward focused, Motivated **Intense Anxiety**: Accomplished, Driven, Frenzied, Vigorous

ANXIETY helps you plan for the future and organize the tasks you need to complete and the deadlines you need to meet. **Note:** If your anxiety has any sense of dread or danger in it, your life-saving emotion of *panic* is involved (see pages 112–121). It's important to learn the difference between these two vital emotions because the practices for them are different!

Anxiety (or worry) is a motivating emotion that's focused on the future: on possible upcoming changes, problems, or opportunities. Anxiety helps you plan, make preparations, organize the tasks you need to complete, and meet your deadlines. Anxiety also supports you when you need to procrastinate.

If there are tasks that you nearly always avoid, how does your anxiety arise to help you get them done?

If there are tasks that you nearly always complete on time, how are they different from the tasks you avoid? What is the emotional atmosphere around each kind of task?

The Important Nuances of Anxiety

As you know, anxiety is a very active emotion. Because it focuses on the future, it can be ungrounding by its very nature as it sort of leans you forward and energizes you. It's helpful to be aware of the intensity of the anxiety you're feeling, so I've described the nuances of anxiety below.

SOFT ANXIETY	MEDIUM ANXIETY	INTENSE ANXIETY
In its *soft* state, your anxiety will gently help you realize what you need to do, and it will help you organize and complete your tasks in an efficient way. When it's in this soft state, you might not even think of it as anxiety!	In its *medium* state, your anxiety will be more insistent, and will probably be obvious to you and to others. You'll feel more of a time crunch, and you might even ignore things that are not related to what needs to be done.	In its *intense* state, your anxiety will help you face a sudden deadline or a mountain of tasks that need to be handled immediately. In these intense situations, you might become frantic or lose your focus.

Repressing your anxiety isn't a good idea because it will keep bubbling up – it has important tasks to complete! However, *expressing* anxiety when it's in an intense feedback loop can be troublesome; it can run you in five different directions at once. A helpful practice is to turn toward your anxiety and ask, *What **truly** needs to be done?*

If you can focus yourself and ask yourself what truly needs to be done, you can bring your full awareness to the situation. When you can learn to recognize your anxiety, center yourself, and engage with it mindfully, you'll have access to its gifts of foresight, planning, and motivation!

The Importance of Procrastination

Many people see procrastination as a problem or a sign of laziness, but the original meaning of procrastination is "belonging to tomorrow," or "deferred until the morning." In many situations, it's important *not* to act, but to wait and let your ideas percolate. Procrastination can give you a breather so that your creativity can flow. If you'd like to explore the genius in procrastination, see my book *Embracing Anxiety*.

 When you procrastinate, what are some of your favorite procrastination activities?

What kinds of relief do these activities provide?

Some Notes about Anxiety

Anxiety is an action-oriented emotion that can intensify quickly. As such, you may miss its softer levels of activation and only feel it when it's more obvious. See the Emotional Vocabulary List on page 163 and choose some words that help you identify your anxiety when it's subtle and easier to work with. This next practice is a specific healing practice for your anxiety from my book *Embracing Anxiety*.

Conscious Questioning for Anxiety

This gentle questioning practice can help you engage directly with your anxiety and identify each of the issues it's responding to so that you can organize all of your tasks, concerns, and ideas. You can begin this practice by asking yourself (out loud) about each of the things that *truly* need to be done.

The word *truly* is key because anxiety is so forward focused that it could send you into a flurry of activity that doesn't actually get you anywhere. Your anxiety brings you a great deal of energy to help you get things done, but it needs your help to organize and focus itself.

It's also very helpful to write things down. Writing is a way to physically express your anxieties, become aware of them, and organize them intentionally. You could create a bullet-pointed list, or you could create a more flowing type of mind map, whichever works best for you.

Simply speaking or writing out your anxieties is an emotionally intelligent action that helps your anxiety organize and focus itself so that you can settle yourself. With this quick and focused awareness practice, you can access the gifts of your anxiety, identify any upcoming tasks, organize everything you need to do to complete those tasks, and support yourself and your anxiety.

How to Consciously Question Your Anxiety

1. Begin your Conscious Questioning session with a clear statement such as "Okay, I'm consciously questioning my anxiety now."

2. Ask your anxiety what *truly* needs to be done right now. Remember to write down the answers! If you need some support, here are some helpful questions you might ask:

   - Have I achieved or completed something similar in the past?

   - What are my strengths and resources?

   - Can I delegate any tasks?

   - Are there any upcoming deadlines?

- Is anything unfinished?

- What do I need to do to prepare?

- What is one small task I can complete right now?

3. When you feel done, end your Conscious Questioning session with a clear statement such as, "Thanks anxiety! I'm done now."

4. When you're done, do one (or more) of the tasks that you and your anxiety have identified, and also do something that's fun, grounding, or soothing.

Take good care of yourself, and remember that anxiety is always looking out for you and trying to help you! Also, this motto from our Dynamic Emotional Integration (DEI) community may be helpful:

There's always enough time for every important thing.

Practices to Help You Work with Your Anxiety

Empathic Mindfulness Practices: Grounding and Focusing ~ Conscious Complaining (solo and with a partner) ~ Conscious Questioning for Anxiety Burning Contracts ~ Renegotiating Contracts ~ Defining Your Boundary Rejuvenation

Additional Practices: Procrastinating intentionally ~ List-making ~ Organizing and planning

It may be useful to circle the practices above that feel supportive to you, or that would have helped the last time you felt very anxious.

Personalizing Your Anxiety Practices

Take a moment to feel into the anxiety questions: *What brought this feeling forward? What **truly** needs to be done?*

Anxiety often needs your help to focus itself clearly, but when your anxiety is highly activated, it may be difficult to focus yourself!

 Take some time when you're **not** highly activated to jot down practices, activities, or people that help you focus when your anxiety needs to arise in its medium or intense states.

MY ANXIETY SUPPORT SYSTEM

Note: If you do what you can to address your anxiety, and it doesn't respond to you, please reach out for help from a counselor or health-care provider. Sometimes, especially with a very active emotion like anxiety, we all need support to bring our emotions back into balance.

Confusion: The Healing Mask for Fear and Anxiety

The Gifts and Skills in Confusion	Soft Awareness ~ Innocence ~ Malleability Obliviousness ~ Taking a pause
The Internal Questions for Confusion	*How can I welcome not-knowing and not-doing?* *What is my intention?*
Some Nuances of Confusion	**Soft Confusion**: Malleable, Open-minded, Pensive, Soft-focused **Medium Confusion:** Confused, Contemplative, Spacious, Unfocused **Intense Confusion:** Befuddled, Mystified, Suspended, Timeless

CONFUSION arises when you're overwhelmed by too much change, too many tasks, or too many options. Confusion is a healing mask for fear and anxiety, and it arises when there's too much input or too many changes.

When you're confused, you can't make decisions because they might not be the right decisions, and you can't move ahead because you might move in the wrong way. This foggy, gauzy state often arises to give you a rest from input and to pull a soft veil over the situations you face. In many cases, confusion arises when your behavior or your plans aren't compatible with who, what, or where you really want to be. Confusion reduces your focus and your decision-making capacities for good reasons.

If you fight your confusion and force yourself to act, you'll almost certainly fall right back into the confusion again (or you'll endlessly second-guess yourself). The practice for confusion is not to erase it or blast your way through it, but to intentionally make room for not-knowing and not-doing.

What is your current attitude toward confusion?

a. If you're fine with being confused, how do you behave when confusion arises?

b. If you struggle with confusion, how do you behave when you feel confused?

Confusion is not the problem; it's *telling* you about the problem! When you're confused, it's very important to understand that an intelligence inside you is working on your behalf. If you can engage with your confusion, you can make space for not-knowing and not-doing and reconnect to your own true intentions again.

Confusion about Choices

When you're confused, it's healing to simply *be confused* and take a break.

However, if you're confused about making important choices, a helpful question to ask yourself is *What is my intention?* This question may help you connect with your needs and values, which are often pushed aside by the bustle of life. Knowing your intentions can help you see what's important and what isn't.

Some Notes about Confusion

Asking the confusion questions may help if you're overwhelmed by a flurry of input or other people's needs. However, consistent confusion may be a sign that you're in an environment that is too activating for you. It may help to keep a confusion journal so that you can track the quality of your focus throughout your day. If your confusion persists, you might want to visit your doctor, because a loss of focus may be a sign of changes in your health. Remember that all emotions are signals; they're not the problem—they *point* to the problem!

Practices to Help You Work with Your Confusion

Empathic Mindfulness Practices: Hands-On Grounding ~ Defining Your Boundary ~ Conscious Complaining (solo and with a partner) ~ Rejuvenation

Additional Practices: Taking a break ~ Resting ~ Doing nothing ~ Daydreaming

It may be useful to circle the practices above that help when you feel confused. Note that confusion doesn't require a lot of intentional practices because it's about taking a break and resting when too much is coming at you.

Personalizing Your Confusion Practices

Take a moment to feel into the first confusion question: *How can I welcome not-knowing and not-doing?*

Most of us have been taught to always know things and always be doing things. We don't have much permission to *not* know or *not* do, and sadly, that will make confusion more necessary and more likely. We need rest and downtime!

 Write down some ways to support yourself and your confusion when it's time to stop and take a complete break.

Now feel into the second confusion question: *What is my intention?*

Connecting with your intentions, especially when you have to make a choice, can help you tune into your enduring values and your intended purpose in this world.

If you're confused about choices, write down your intentions **first** (you can also rely on the list of things you value from the Anger section). Then compare each of the confusing choices to your stated intentions and values.

MY INTENTIONS AND VALUES	CHOICE 1	CHOICE 2

This practice can help you reconnect to yourself, especially in a swirl of obligations, time constraints, conflicting choices, and too-muchness.

Jealousy: Relational Radar

The Gifts and Skills in Jealousy	Love ~ Commitment ~ Intimacy Security ~ Connection ~ Loyalty Fairness
The Internal Questions for Jealousy	*What kinds of intimacy do I desire and want to offer?* *What betrayals must be recognized and healed?*
Some Nuances of Jealousy	**Soft Jealousy:** Concerned, Connected, Insecure, Vulnerable **Medium Jealousy:** Distrustful, Jealous, Lonely, Loving **Intense Jealousy:** Ardent, Lustful, Passionate, Possessive

JEALOUSY helps you notice and address challenges that may threaten your connection to love, loyalty, or security in your relationships. Jealousy is a combination of intuition (fear) and self-protection (anger) that arises when your most intimate relationships are challenged. These challenges may come from external sources, from an internal lack of self-worth, or both.

The key to working with your jealousy is to identify when the risks you sense come from an actual betrayal, and when they come from your own sense of unworthiness or insecurity.

In either case, it's important to address these issues.

Think about a past relationship where you felt jealous.

     a. As you look back, was the jealousy alerting you to disloyalty in your partner? If so, what were the signs?

     b. If not, was it alerting you to a sense of your own insecurity?

Healthy and committed relationships are vital to your social and emotional well-being and survival. If your mate is unreliable, or if your relationship is in question, your jealousy will arise to help you face this very real threat to your well-being. This is a necessary and healthy response. However, if you don't listen to and honor your jealousy, it may pull you into a feedback loop of suspicion and insecurity that can disturb you and the people in your life.

Listen to your jealousy; it arises for a valid reason. Ignoring it is like throwing a noisy smoke alarm out of the window before finding out why it went off!

 If you're in a relationship today where you feel jealous, what insights is your jealousy bringing you about your relationship? Or about yourself?

You need security and loyalty in your most important relationships. If you ignore your jealousy, you'll have trouble identifying and maintaining reliable relationship partners. Luckily, when your jealousy is free-flowing, you won't appear obsessively jealous or possessive; rather, your natural intuition and clear boundaries will help you choose, nurture, and hold on to trustworthy mates and friends.

Some Notes about Jealousy

Jealousy is a brilliant social emotion that keeps tabs on every aspect of your important relationships. Your jealousy will not only monitor your relationships, but it will make sure that *you* remain loyal and connected to the important people in your life.

Sadly, this emotion is repressed and hated by most people, so a great deal of its genius is trapped in the shadows, where it can become toxic. Most of us also have no practice at all for this emotion, so you'll need support to identify all of the issues that your jealousy is pointing to *before* you speak with your partner about them. The practice of Ethical Empathic Gossip will help you access jealousy's genius in ethical and healing ways.

Practices to Help You Work with Your Jealousy

Empathic Mindfulness Practices: Ethical Empathic Gossip ~ Grounding and Focusing ~ Defining Your Boundary ~ Rejuvenation ~ Conscious Complaining (solo and with a partner) ~ Burning Contracts ~ Renegotiating Contracts

Additional Practices: Identifying your intimacy needs and the needs of your partner(s) ~ Exploring information about healthy relationships

It may be useful to circle the practices above that help you and your jealousy figure out what's bothering you.

Personalizing Your Jealousy Practices

Take a moment to feel into the jealousy questions: *What kinds of intimacy do I desire and want to offer? What betrayals must be recognized and healed?*

Jealousy is a social emotion that watches over your intimate relationships, which means that it contains a great deal of information about you and your relationships.

It can be helpful to write down a list of the kinds of intimacy you'd like to receive and what kinds you can offer. This can have a grounding and boundary-setting effect on you and your jealousy so that you can understand what's present and what's missing in your relationships, or what betrayals (of your needs or yourself) may have occurred.

THE INTIMACY I WANT	THE INTIMACY I OFFER

Envy: Interactional Radar

The Gifts and Skills in Envy	Fairness ~ Equity ~ Access to resources and recognition ~ Generosity ~ Security
The Internal Questions for Envy	*What resources and security do I desire for myself and others?* *What inequalities must be made right?*
Some Nuances of Envy	**Soft Envy**: Fair, Inspired, Protective, Wanting **Medium Envy**: Covetous, Generous, Envious, Equitable **Intense Envy**: Affluent, Deprived, Grasping, Greedy

ENVY helps you notice and address challenges that may threaten your material security, resources, and/or recognition. Envy is similar to jealousy in that it contains a mixture of boundary-restoring anger and intuitive fear. The difference between these two emotions is that envy watches over your material security and your access to resources and recognition, while your jealousy watches over the quality of love and loyalty in your close relationships.

Some people see envy as a primitive emotion. They mistakenly think that some emotions are no longer necessary. However, in our modern world, we now require much more money and resources than our ancestors ever did – just to feed ourselves! This means that the deep and protective wisdom in envy is now even more necessary for our survival. Envy keeps us safely connected to the social and material support we need to live and flourish.

Many children are trained out of their envy by well-meaning parents and teachers who force them to share their toys, take turns, or otherwise feel ashamed about their own wants and desires.

When you were little, were you allowed to have a say about your own things and your own desires?

      a. If so, how does your envy work in your life now?

      b. If not, how do you and your envy respond to your needs and desires today?

Envy is a vital and necessary emotion. If you don't work well with your envy – if you suppress it or let it go wild – you (and everyone around you) will be disrupted by your attempts to either receive as little as possible or grab whatever you can get your hands on. When you work well with your envy, it will make sure that you're safe and well-positioned socially, and it will also make sure that there is enough for everyone else.

When you learn to channel your envy honorably, you won't appear greedy *or* self-abandoning. Instead, your envy will give you the strength and insight you need to understand your social world and work well within it.

When you learn how to work with your envy, it will help you access what you need and celebrate the successes and gains of others without ignoring your own needs for security and success.

Think about someone you envy today. Describe them, or the situation around them. What is your envy showing you about what you admire in this person (or what you desire for yourself)?

Some Notes about Envy

Envy contains deep and rich amounts of information about your social world and everyone in it, but because envy (like jealousy) is repressed and hated, its information tends to live in the shadows, where it can become self-serving or spiteful.

However, like jealousy, your envy gathers essential information about your social world, and it contains astonishing amounts of genius. The Ethical Empathic Gossip practice can help you access envy's vital social information in healthy and ethical ways.

Practices to Help You Work with Your Envy

Empathic Mindfulness Practices: Ethical Empathic Gossip ~ Grounding and Focusing ~ Defining Your Boundary ~ Rejuvenation ~ Conscious Complaining (solo and with a partner) ~ Burning Contracts ~ Renegotiating Contracts

Additional Practices: Identifying your needs and the needs of the people around you ~ Learning about finances ~ Learning about social structure

It may be useful to circle the practices above that help when you feel envious.

Personalizing Your Envy Practices

Take a moment to feel into the envy questions: *What resources and security do I desire for myself and others? What inequalities must be made right?*

Like jealousy, envy is a brilliant social emotion that gathers an astonishing amount of information about the security and equality that are present (or absent) in your social world.

Be aware: If you spend time on social media, watch how your envy is manipulated and inflated by advertisers and influencers. The practice below can help you focus your envy on your true and enduring values, which can protect you from manipulation.

 It can be healing and protective to write down a list of your desires in regard to what kinds of resources and security are important to you (and what you would like others to have as well). This can have a grounding and boundary-setting effect so that you can focus on your deepest values that support true security and equality for all.

What I Desire and Require	What I Desire for Others

Immediate Panic: The Powerful Protector

The Gifts and Skills in Immediate Panic	Sudden energy ~ Fixed attention ~ Absolute stillness ~ Survival instincts
The Internal Questions for Immediate Panic	*What is currently a threat?* *How can I fight, flee, freeze, or flock to safety?*
Some Nuances of Immediate Panic	**Soft Immediate Panic**: Apprehensive, Aware, Cautious, Oriented **Medium Immediate Panic**: Alarmed, Safety seeking, Ready, Resourceful **Intense Immediate Panic:** Laser focused, Hyperactivated, Panicked, Survival focused

IMMEDIATE PANIC is a powerful emotion that arises in response to a direct threat to your physical life. Immediate panic helps you fight, flee, freeze, or flock to safety. If you trust your instincts and listen to your body, your panic will choose the right response pretty much every time.

Immediate panic can help you fight or flee during your ordeal (if you can, or if it's a good survival strategy), or it may help you freeze. Your panic may also help you flock together with others for safety. Panic may also release pain-killing endorphins that will help you survive injury, or freeze and dissociate if you need to. Each of these actions requires energy, which panic supplies in abundance.

After the ordeal is over, your immediate panic will retreat, and you'll need to cool down and down-regulate from all of this activation. You may need to shake and tremble all over, replay the ordeal in any number of ways, talk to someone you trust, and reintegrate yourself.

Recall two situations where your fight, flee, freeze, or flock-to-safety behaviors kept you safe from harm, and list them here.

If you remember, describe how you settled yourself after one or both of these survival situations.

If you don't make time for this cool-down period, you may remain in a hyperactivated state, which your panic may take as a sign that you're still in danger and requiring its help. This hyperactivation can begin to cycle into flashbacks and post-traumatic replays of the original ordeal. We call this *frozen panic*, and you can read about its healing purpose in the Frozen Panic section.

Some Notes about Immediate Panic

There's been a lot of focus on *frozen panic* over the past years, and it has sort of hidden our awareness of immediate panic, which often works very gently to keep us safe. For instance, if a ball or item comes flying at you, and you get out of its way, that's immediate panic helping you. Panic doesn't have to be dramatic, and it doesn't have to be a long-lasting emotion.

Keep an eye out for the soft levels of immediate panic as you go through your days. It's the emotion that keeps you safe from harm!

Practices to Help You Work with Your Immediate Panic

Empathic Mindfulness Practices: Grounding and Focusing ~ Hands-On Grounding ~ Defining Your Boundary

Additional Practices: Listening to your body ~ Maintaining your strength and agility ~ Taking martial arts or self-defense training

It may be useful to circle the practices above that help you work with your immediate panic.

Personalizing Your Immediate Panic Practices

Take a moment to feel into the immediate panic questions: *What is currently a threat? How can I fight, flee, freeze, or flock to safety?*

Working with your immediate panic doesn't require a lot of practices; it's a deeply instinctual, lifesaving, and fast-moving emotion! It often acts before you can think, and thank goodness for that.

Because immediate panic is a member of the fear family, the fear practice of creating space to listen to your instincts will help. It's also helpful to write down instances where your immediate panic stepped forward to protect you. This can help you learn to identify and connect to its genius and support its essential work.

The Situation	My Panic's Response	The Skills I Developed

Frozen Panic: The Healing Witness

The Gifts and Skills in Frozen Panic	Healing from past traumas ~ Freedom from cycling patterns ~ Reintegration
The Internal Questions for Frozen Panic	*What has been frozen in time?* *What **healing** action must be taken?*
Some Nuances of Frozen Panic	**Soft Frozen Panic**: Disconcerted, Fidgety, Leery, Uneasy **Medium Frozen Panic**: Jumpy, Shaky, Suspicious, Unnerved **Intense Frozen Panic**: Dissociated, Paralyzed, Healing from trauma, Violent

FROZEN PANIC arises to help you address unhealed traumas, and it brings you the energy you need to create healing and resolution. The key is to take *healing* actions with the energy panic brings to you. Remember: you've already survived, and frozen panic can help you renegotiate your traumatic ordeals and move from basic survival into resilience and wholeness.

If you weren't able to cool down after a traumatic experience, you may remain in a constant state of alarm and readiness, and you may find yourself jumping, startling, and striking out randomly. Your body might not be able to relax, your sleep may become disturbed, and your self-care habits may fall away. You may also begin to cycle through memories of the panic-inducing situation in a way that seems obsessive: you may experience persistent flashbacks, nightmares, phantom pains, disorientation, emotional volatility or numbness, and any number of behavioral disruptions. Yet here, in the territory of frozen panic, is the entryway to reintegration and healing.

The second question for frozen panic – *What **healing** action must be taken?* – is crucial because panic brings you so much energy that you could take literally hundreds of actions. But would they be *healing* actions? This chart, modified from my book *Embracing Anxiety*, explores the difference between healing actions that help you work with your frozen panic versus dubious actions that will likely increase your frozen panic.

Healing Actions to Address Frozen Panic	Dubious Actions to Avoid Frozen Panic
Grounding and soothing yourself	Ignoring your body and your needs
Finding trauma-informed therapy	Toughing it out and suffering alone
Reaching out for loving support	Pushing people away
Eating nourishing food on a regular schedule	Overeating to numb yourself, obsessing on the perfect diet, undereating, forgetting to eat, or avoiding food
Developing a regular and healing movement practice	Becoming immobile or using exercise to distract yourself, burn off your panic, or exhaust yourself
Practicing Rejuvenation	Using substances, distractions, or dissociation to achieve a moment of peace, relief, or happiness

HEALING ACTIONS TO ADDRESS FROZEN PANIC	DUBIOUS ACTIONS TO AVOID FROZEN PANIC
Practicing Conscious Complaining	Complaining unconsciously or silencing yourself because no one will listen anyway
Practicing Defining Your Boundary	Letting circumstances or other people set your boundaries for you
Finding a supportive community of people who are working on similar challenges	Isolating yourself or convincing yourself that healing isn't possible
Choosing healthy relationship partners who are safe, soothing, and loving	Choosing unavailable or unstable partners who activate your panic response

It's important to observe any of your dubious actions with compassion. Most of us not only didn't learn how to work with frozen panic, but we also didn't even know what it was! Congratulate yourself for getting through life in whatever way you could and support yourself by trying some of the healing actions above (or creating your own) to see if they work for you.

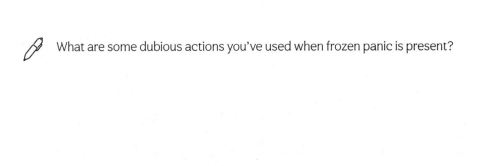 What are some dubious actions you've used when frozen panic is present?

What are some healing actions you could try to see if they help?

We're all learning and moving toward integration, and the dubious actions kept us going, so thanks are in order. These dubious actions are examples of what George Bonanno calls "coping ugly" in his excellent book *The End of Trauma*. It's a very helpful book to read as you learn how to work with frozen panic and reframe your approach to traumatizing ordeals.

I also learned how to work with frozen panic in a book by Peter Levine called *Waking the Tiger*. His work, Somatic Experiencing® (see traumahealing.org), taught me how to approach my after-panic state in the way healthy animals do, and it's not only empowering, but it also helps retrieve the genius of frozen panic.

Gather Support as You Work with Frozen Panic

Because frozen panic points to an unhealed trauma, it's important to gather support as you work with it. The panic chapter in *The Language of Emotions* has many suggestions, and there's a trauma healing topic in the Resources section at the end of this workbook.

You may need counseling or medical support as you heal, but know that frozen panic has a vital purpose. Frozen panic didn't *create* the trauma; it's *pointing to* the trauma, and it can help you resolve it.

Some Notes about Frozen Panic

Trauma is not a life sentence, and if you can lean into the healing genius of your frozen panic, you can regulate and reintegrate yourself. As you work with your frozen panic cycles, movement can help you heal and restore yourself. Dance, free-form movement, yoga, tai chi, water workouts, hiking, biking, and sports can help you restore your flexibility, your strength, and your playfulness again.

Practices to Help You Work with Your Frozen Panic

Empathic Mindfulness Practices: Grounding and Focusing ~ Hands-On Grounding ~ Defining Your Boundary ~ Rejuvenation ~ Burning Contracts Renegotiating Contracts

Additional Practices: Choosing healing actions ~ Exploring somatic trauma-healing therapies ~ Choosing healing movement practices

It may help you to circle the practices above that feel supportive or that would help you work with your frozen panic.

Personalizing Your Frozen Panic Practices

Take a moment to feel into the frozen panic questions: *What has been frozen in time? What **healing** action must be taken?*

As you may know, frozen panic responses can feel unsettling or even overwhelming. It's very tempting to try to avoid the whole situation, but these panic responses are a necessary part of coming back from unresolved traumatic situations and reintegrating yourself. Surrounding yourself with support is an important part of unfreezing these responses and healing.

 Take some time to write down the personal healing actions you like best (you can take some cues from the healing actions table on pages 117-118 and your answer to the question on page 119) so that you have many resources to rely on when your frozen panic needs your attention and support.

THE SADNESS FAMILY
Stopping, Letting Go, and Recovering

Sadness ~ Grief ~ Depression ~ The Suicidal Urge

The emotions in the sadness family help you release things
that aren't working and mourn things that are gone so
that you can relax, let go, and rejuvenate yourself.

Sadness: The Water Bearer

The Gifts and Skills in Sadness	Release ~ Fluidity ~ Grounding ~ Relaxation Rejuvenation
The Internal Questions for Sadness	*What must be released?* *What must be rejuvenated?*
Some Nuances of Sadness	**Soft Sadness**: Disappointed, Grounded, Low, Relaxed **Medium Sadness:** Down, Rejuvenated, Sad, Soothed **Intense Sadness:** Despairing, Forlorn, Inconsolable, Released

SADNESS helps you let go of things, ideas, and relationships that aren't working any longer. People often blame sadness for the way they're feeling; however, sadness arises in response to the fact that they're holding on to something that doesn't work. This something might be an attitude, a relationship, a belief, or a behavior that may have worked in the past, but doesn't work anymore. Sadness arises to help us let go. When we can let go, we'll finally be able to relax and recover.

Sadly, many people equate sadness with weakness, and when they feel sad, they repress it and become inflexible. Or when they witness sadness in others, they try to squash it or shame people out of it.

Many of us have been taught to repress sadness and adopt a tough or super-competent exterior. When your sadness arises, how do you usually behave?

What does your boundary look and feel like when you repress your sadness?

What does your boundary look and feel like when you can relax and let go of things that aren't working?

The next time you feel sad, observe your reaction. Do you distract yourself or shame yourself when your tears and sadness try to come forward? If so, it may be time to burn or renegotiate some contracts (see pages 55-61) related to your treatment of sadness. Most of us have had pretty terrible training about sadness, but luckily, you can create a welcoming home for sadness in the privacy of your own emotional realm.

You can also honor your sadness even when you're in the presence of sadness repressors. If it's not safe or acceptable to cry or show sadness openly, it's fine to repress your obvious sadness. However, you can still honor sadness and remain emotionally honest. You can inhale, soften your posture, and let go of tension as you exhale.

This is not the same as a good cry, but it is a way to honor your sadness and your need to let go when you're in an emotionally repressive environment.

 Think back to a recent time when you felt sad but didn't know why. Can you feel into what your sadness was helping you release?

Sadness isn't just about loss and letting go. It's also about restoring your flow and your ease so that you can reset yourself. When you can finally let go of things that simply don't work anymore, you'll suddenly have room for things that *do* work.

Some Notes about Sadness

I call sadness "the all-purpose healing balm of the soul" because it has the power to ground and soothe you in any situation. If you experience any form of tension or hyperactivation, your sadness can help you relax and settle yourself.

Welcome sadness in yourself and others. When people around you need to cry, don't stop them or turn away in embarrassment. Just breathe in, relax, and create a welcoming space for the essential healing balm of sadness.

Practices to Help You Work with Your Sadness

Empathic Mindfulness Practices: Grounding and Focusing ~ Hands-On Grounding ~ Burning Contracts ~ Rejuvenation

Additional Practices: Letting go ~ Crying ~ Relaxing ~ Softening your posture Soothing yourself

It may help you to circle the practices above that support you when you feel sad.

Personalizing Your Sadness Practices

Take a moment to feel into the sadness questions: *What must be released? What must be rejuvenated?*

Sadness is about learning to let go and flow so that you have the space you need to relax and rejuvenate yourself. However, our modern lives tend to push us to work endlessly, never rest, and accumulate more and more things and experiences. In this type of go-go-go environment, your sadness needs support!

 Create a list of sadness-supporting influences and activities for yourself (such as slow dancing, listening to music, resting, clearing out clutter, etc.) so that you can drop into the healing waters of sadness whenever you need to.

How I Support My Sadness and Flow

Grief: The Deep River of the Soul

The Gifts and Skills in Grief	Mourning ~ Remembrance ~ Honoring of loss Deep release ~ Lamentation
The Internal Questions for Grief	*What must be mourned?* *How do I honor what was lost?*
Some Nuances of Grief	**Soft Grief**: Contemplative, Disconnected, Releasing, Wistful **Medium Grief:** Dispirited, Grieving, Lamenting, Remembering **Intense Grief:** Anguished, Bereaved, Heartbroken, Sanctified

GRIEF supports you when you've lost something essential – a person, a relationship, an item, or a situation – that will never come back. Grief is an essential part of love.

Grief is a beautiful emotion, and it's very different from sadness. With sadness, you have a choice about letting go, but with grief, you have no choice. The loss occurs without your permission, and it is permanent. Grief is a powerful emotion because it comes to help you face powerful losses.

Identifying the Difference between Sadness and Grief

The table on the next page provides two examples of the difference between sadness and grief, and room for you to add your own examples.

SADNESS: THAT WHICH I CAN CHOOSE TO LET GO	GRIEF: THAT WHICH HAS BEEN LOST FOREVER
Clutter in the kitchen	My grandfather
My avoidance of exercise	My chance to become a professional athlete

Your grief may arise in response to the loss of a relationship, a dream, a job, your health, or an important possession. You may also feel grief after a betrayal, or in response to never having had something that others take for granted. When these losses occur, grief helps you reach the deepest places in yourself where you can let go and mourn so that your healing can begin.

Grief does not *bring* you pain; it is a response to painful losses. If you avoid and repress your grief by refusing to feel or acknowledge it, each death and each loss will just stack itself on top of the last one – like papers on a disorganized desk – until you're filled with unfelt and unresolved losses. If you welcome your grief, stay grounded, and listen to your body, you'll be able to feel your way through and make it to the other side.

The process of grieving is individual; each of us has our own ways, ideas, and timelines that work for us. Some people grieve well alone, but in most cultures, grief is a communal process. It can be very healing to experience grief rituals in diverse cultures and find ones that speak to your soul.

 Do you or your family have any supportive practices for grief?

    a. If so, what are the elements of these practices?

    b. If not, how do you grieve?

Are you a part of a culture that ritualizes grief in helpful ways?

    a. If so, how do these rituals support you?

If you don't have access to healing grief rituals, see the books of Megan Devine, find a local grief support group, or join us at Empathy Academy for our yearly online grief ritual.

When you're done grieving (for now; grief often returns to remind you of the importance of what you've lost), you won't need or want to erase the memory of your loss; instead, your loss will become a part of you – a part of your history, your strength, and your awareness of life's fragility. When you honor and welcome your grief, you won't become bulletproof or grief-hardened; instead, you'll soften into the true strength that arises when you connect to grief and loss in sacred ways.

Some Notes about Grief

Joy can arise alongside or after grief, because both emotions are involved in times of communion and deep connection. As you mourn and grieve, joy may arise to support you as you face the deep and healing waters of grief.

In DEI, we learn about grief rituals, shrines, and altars that can bring sacredness and community to the process of grieving. If you're struggling with grief or ungrieved losses, a DEI professional (see our international directory at empathyacademy.org) can help you create a grief ritual so that you can mourn, heal, and reintegrate yourself with support and companionship.

Practices to Help You Work with Your Grief

Empathic Mindfulness Practices: Grounding and Focusing ~ Hands-On Grounding ~ Rejuvenation

Additional Practices: Crying ~ Mourning ~ Creating or attending grief rituals Joining a grief support group ~ Memorializing your loss

It may be useful to circle the practices above that feel supportive when you're grieving.

Personalizing Your Grief Practices

Take a moment to feel into the grief questions: *What must be mourned? How do I honor what was lost?*

Many people avoid grief because facing their losses feels overwhelming. However, losses are necessary parts of a life that's fully lived.

 It can be healing to list what you've lost and include the activities you've created (or wish to create) to help you honor your losses.

What I've Lost	How I Honor My Loss

Situational Depression: Ingenious Stagnation

The Gifts and Skills in Situational Depression	Inward focus ~ Stillness ~ Awareness of imbalance ~ Purposeful inaction Reconnection with yourself ~ Reality check
The Internal Questions for Situational Depression	*Where has my energy gone?* *Why was it sent away?*
Some Nuances of Situational Depression	**Soft Depression**: Apathetic, Disinterested, Flat, Realistic **Medium Depression:** Constantly Irritated, Angry, or Enraged (see the anger section), Depressed, Inward focused **Intense Depression:** Anguished, Self-destructive, Tormented, Transformed

SITUATIONAL DEPRESSION arises when some aspect of your life is unbalanced or dysfunctional, and it withholds your energy for vital reasons. Situational depression has a purpose, which is to alert you that something is wrong and to prevent you from moving forward until you address the situation. Your job is to find out what that situation is.

If you study your life carefully, you can observe your physical health, your relationships, your work environment, and your social situation and discover if there's trouble in any of these areas. (See the Depression Inventory on my website at karlamclaren.com/LoE-workbook for a supportive checklist.)

Sometimes, the cause of your depression will be very clear, yet there will be nothing you can do to address it. Even so, there are many ways to support yourself as you wait for the depressing situation to resolve (or as you plan your escape from it).

Conscious Complaining with a Partner (see pages 48-50) can be very helpful for situational depression. It can help you talk openly about the problems and get a clearer handle on the issues. List a few people you'd like to complain with when you're feeling low and stuck.

Distracting activities like watching TV, playing video games, or comfort eating can help you live with and around situational depression. Artistic expression and movement can be amazingly helpful, and you can sometimes find ideas or answers through these forms of expression.

Connecting with restful and funny people is also wonderful, and being in nature or connecting with art, music, poetry, or great thinkers are excellent ways to care for yourself in response to depressing situations that you cannot resolve just yet.

List some activities that support you when you feel low and drained.

Situational depression can feel similar to apathy (or boredom). If you have experience with both of these emotions, can you describe the difference between apathy and depression?

Some Notes about Situational Depression

Situational depression is a low mood that tracks to something you can address with changes to your lifestyle or behavior. However, there are many other forms of depression, and they may require therapeutic and/or medical intervention. If your depression is cyclical, or if it doesn't respond to healing changes you make, please seek therapeutic support (see the Resources section at the end of this workbook).

Also note that in some people, depression is accompanied by irritation, frustration, and even rage. What looks like a problem with anger may actually be a sign of depression. The Depression Inventory on my website can help you track and observe the depressing influences in your life. If you study the inventory and cannot identify any imbalance or any apparent reason for your depression, please seek therapeutic support to help you explore the underlying causes.

Practices to Help You Work with Your Situational Depression

Empathic Mindfulness Practices: Grounding and Focusing ~ Hands-On Grounding ~ Defining Your Boundary ~ Conscious Complaining (solo and with a partner) ~ Burning Contracts ~ Renegotiating Contracts ~ Rejuvenation

Additional Practices: Resting ~ Choosing intentionally distracting activities (see the Depression Inventory on my website) ~ Doing nothing, intentionally

It may be useful to circle the practices above that help when you're feeling depressed.

Personalizing Your Situational Depression Practices

Take a moment to feel into the situational depression questions: *Where has my energy gone? Why was it sent away?*

Many of us feel a sense of shame or dejection when we're depressed, as if depression is a character flaw instead of a necessary response to serious problems. Instead of criticizing yourself when you're depressed, you can take an inventory of what's going on around you.

Please remember that depression is not a commentary about your value as a person. Situational depression can help you identify where the problems are so that you can begin to address them.

When you feel depressed, place a checkmark beside any area of your life that is currently troubled or neglected.

My Depression Inventory

Your Body	Your Relationships	Your World
☐ Diet	☐ Your mate (or lack thereof)	☐ Your financial condition
☐ Health	☐ Family	☐ Your employment situation
☐ Exercise	☐ Friends	☐ Your community's condition
☐ Sleep	☐ Colleagues	☐ Your political situation

When you're dealing with a lot of trouble, your situational depression will impede you from moving forward because it's not *time* to move forward. Something is in the way. See the Depression Inventory on my website for ways to support yourself when your situational depression needs to impede your forward movement for important reasons.

The Suicidal Urge: The Darkness Before Dawn

The Gifts and Skills in the Suicidal Urge	Certainty ~ Resolve ~ Liberty ~ Transformation Rebirth
The Internal Questions for the Suicidal Urge	*What behavior or situation must end now?* *What can no longer be tolerated in my soul?*
Some Nuances of the Suicidal Urge	**Soft Suicidal Urges**: Dispirited, Fed up, Resolute, Withdrawn **Medium Suicidal Urges:** Desolate, Emancipated, Fatalistic, Passionless **Intense Suicidal Urges:** Agonized, Death seeking, Freed, Suicidal

SUICIDAL URGES arise when the difference between who you are in your deepest self and who you've become in this world is so extreme that it can no longer be tolerated. Suicidal urges are an emergency message from lost parts of your psyche. These urges want freedom from the life you're living, *but they absolutely do not need your physical life to end.*

If you or anyone you know is feeling suicidal, please know that you're not alone and that free help is always available. Please reach out. In the US, you can text the Suicide and Crisis Lifeline at 988 or call 1-800-273-TALK (8255) or visit their website at suicidepreventionlifeline.org/talk-to-someone-now/. In Canada, text or call 988. For other countries, the International Association for Suicide Prevention at iasp.info/crisis-centres-helplines/ has a list of crisis and suicide prevention centers throughout the world.

Suicidal urges arise in a range of intensities, but if you're feeling any level of suicidal urges right now, don't feel as if you must wait until you're in dire need to reach out for help. If you can learn to identify and get support for your suicidal urges when they're subtle, you may be able to avoid falling into a pit of despair.

If you struggle with suicidal urges, it's important to learn to identify them when they're soft and subtle.

 Think of a time when you felt so fed up with something that you just couldn't tolerate it anymore. Or think of a time when you felt like giving up completely on something or someone. Feel into that situation now: can you identify the serious problems your soft suicidal urge was alerting you to?

Your soft suicidal urge can also help you say an absolute, final NO to a bad situation, a damaging behavior, or a troubling person. Think back to a time when you were able to end a bad situation or relationship with certainty and finality. Where did your strength and certainty come from?

Some Notes about Suicidal Urges

Suicidal urges often travel alongside many trapped emotions and traumatic memories; it's therefore vital to know how to work well with all of your other emotions. It's also important to have the mindfulness practices and resources you need to enter this territory safely. Make sure that you have the support of a counselor and/or your doctor if you need it, and that you can ground and focus yourself and work well with your boundaries.

Suicidal urges often arise at the end of a long struggle, and they can truly be the darkness before the dawn, but they require support. If you're feeling suicidal, please reach out. We need you in this world.

Practices to Help You Work with Your Suicidal Urge

Empathic Mindfulness Practices: Burning Contracts ~ Renegotiating Contracts Grounding and Focusing ~ Hands-On Grounding ~ Defining Your Boundary Conscious Complaining (solo and with a partner) ~ Rejuvenation

Additional Practices: Understanding that your physical life does *not* need to end ~ Saying an absolute NO to unworkable situations ~ Resting ~ Reaching out to a crisis line or counselor (see also the Depression Inventory on my website) Developing a strong emotional vocabulary

It may be useful to circle the practices above that feel supportive when your suicidal urge arises. Know that self-harm is *not at all* what this emotion requires. Instead, your suicidal urge can help you bring a strong and decisive end to unworkable behaviors and free yourself from unlivable situations.

Personalizing Your Suicidal Urge Practices

Take a moment to feel into the suicidal urge questions: *What behavior or situation must end now? What can no longer be tolerated in my soul?*

As it is with situational depression, many of us treat the suicidal urge as a character flaw instead of an essential emotion that arises when things have gotten completely out of hand. A helpful healing practice is to keep an eye on situations or behaviors that are leading you into trouble. You can rely on the soft vocabulary words for the suicidal urge so that you can catch things before they spiral out of control.

 Feel into the soft vocabulary words in the first column below, and circle any that you feel. Then identify the situation or behavior and answer the questions in the second and third columns.

Soft Suicidal Urges	What Needs to End?	What Support Do You Need?
Apathetic Discouraged Disinterested Dispirited ~ Fed up Flat ~ Humorless Indifferent ~ Isolated Pessimistic Purposeless ~ Realistic Resolute ~ Withdrawn World-weary		

If you can learn to catch your suicidal urges when they're in this soft stage, you can often stop yourself from falling into anguish or harming yourself. In the territory of the suicidal urge, your capacity for emotional awareness and sensitivity can literally save your life! If you or anyone you know is feeling suicidal, remember that free and confidential help is always available.

THE HAPPINESS FAMILY
Hope, Confidence, and Inspiration

Happiness ~ Contentment ~ Joy

The emotions in the happiness family help you look around, at yourself, or toward the future with hope, satisfaction, and delight.

Happiness: Amusement and Possibilities

The Gifts and Skills in Happiness	Merriment ~ Amusement ~ Hope Delight ~ Playfulness ~ Invigoration
The Internal Questions for Happiness	*What delights me?* *What makes me feel hopeful?*
Some Nuances of Happiness	**Soft Happiness**: Hopeful, Naïve, Smiling, Upbeat **Medium Happiness:** Delighted, Happy, Optimistic, Playful **Intense Happiness:** Flighty, Giddy, Gullible, Jubilant

HAPPINESS helps you look inside yourself, around you, and toward the future with hope and delight. Your task, when happiness arises naturally, is to laugh, smile, and dream – and then to flow into your next task or your next emotion. Happiness tends to be everyone's favorite emotion, but it's simply one emotion that arises for its own reasons and then goes on its way. Trying to be happy all of the time or forcing it to linger will throw your entire emotional life out of balance.

The key to working with happiness in a healthy way is to see it as a momentary passage and not as a final destination. Flow is the key!

 What are some places, activities, people, or animals that help you feel happy?

Some people avoid happiness because it's often linked with foolishness or silliness (happy fool, slaphappy, etc.) or is treated as a child's emotion. Many of us have been told that hardworking and responsible people must sacrifice happiness.

But there's a flaw in these ideas because children are actually very serious and hardworking. If you've ever built a fort with a group of eight-year-olds or helped a child with a challenging piece of homework, you'll have seen a work ethic that can far exceed that of many adults.

Children have a natural ability to focus themselves on huge problems and projects, yet not feel crushed. Being allowed to laugh, play, and fool around actually helps kids flow into and out of struggles, yet remain focused and energetic.

 Do you make regular time to fool around, play, daydream, or imagine a happy future?

    a. If yes, where did you learn to welcome happiness?

    b. If no, how do you approach life without regular access to your happiness?

We all need play and silliness to balance out our intensity and seriousness. If you allow your happiness to flow freely, it will arise at the correct intensity and at the right time.

If you cannot access happiness when you want to, focus on the healing balm of sadness, which can help you restore your flow. If happiness is regularly inaccessible to you, see the Depression Inventory on my website at karlamclaren.com/LoE-workbook.

Some Notes about Happiness

There's a downside to happiness that's overlooked by people who think that happiness is the best or only emotion to have. Too much focus on happiness can lead to a too-optimistic outlook. This can mean that people will not check in with their other emotions before acting, and therefore will not understand the entire situation or their limitations. As it is with all of your other emotions, balance and flow are key.

Practices to Help You Work with Your Happiness

Empathic Mindfulness Practices: Grounding and Focusing ~ Conscious Complaining (solo and with a partner) ~ Renegotiating Contracts ~ Rejuvenation

Additional Practices: Laughter ~ Play ~ Fun movement practices ~ Being silly

It may be useful to circle the practices above that help you feel and explore your happiness.

Personalizing Your Happiness Practices

Take a moment to feel into the happiness questions: *What delights me? What makes me feel hopeful?*

It can be helpful to remind yourself about activities, ideas, things, and people that help you access your delight and hopefulness. We often get so wrapped up in work, responsibilities, and troubles that we forget about the simple things that help us feel upbeat and playful.

 Use the space below to jot down some happiness reminders for yourself.

MY HAPPINESS LIST

Contentment: Appreciation and Recognition

The Gifts and Skills in Contentment	Satisfaction ~ Self-esteem ~ Confidence Renewal ~ Fulfillment ~ Enjoyment
The Internal Question for Contentment	*How have I embodied my authentic values?*
Some Nuances of Contentment	**Soft Contentment:** Calm, Comfortable, Encouraged, Self-aware **Medium Contentment:** Confident, Contented, Fulfilled, Proud **Intense Contentment:** Arrogant, Overconfident, Satisfied, Self-absorbed

CONTENTMENT helps you celebrate your healthy behaviors, your achievements, and your willingness to challenge yourself. Contentment arises when you're living up to your own expectations and your internal moral code, or when you've done an excellent job. When they're working well together, your contentment and your shame partner up to help you manage your behavior in ways that support grounded and realistic self-esteem.

If your shame is too intense, or you're dealing with unhealthy shaming messages, you may have difficulty feeling contentment. You may feel as if nothing you do is ever right. On the other hand, if you don't have *enough* shame, you may feel contentment for no good reason, and you may develop inflated self-esteem. When these two emotions are out of balance, you might have difficulty managing your behavior, your self-esteem, or your ability to change and grow.

Contentment is connected to feeling proud of yourself, but sadly, pride is treated as a negative trait. When you were young, were you allowed to feel proud of yourself?

a. If yes, what is your relationship to contentment and self-esteem today?

b. If no, are you able to feel proud of yourself today? What accomplishments help you feel contented with yourself?

Sadly, some people avoid contentment because they think it's vain or arrogant to celebrate themselves. However, contentment gives you the permission and courage you need to challenge yourself and strive for difficult goals. If you don't welcome your contentment, you may not be able to identify or appreciate your hard work or your talents.

On the other hand, trying to force your contentment is not healthy. Research has suggested that people with low self-esteem actually feel *worse* after repeating positive affirmations or phrases that are supposed to make them feel better about themselves. Your shame and your contentment can't be fooled by false statements.

The key to a healthy relationship with your contentment is to take time to acknowledge yourself when you're living up to your values and when you've done good work – and then return to the work that will lead to contentment again!

A Simple Way to Observe Your Contentment

Discovering your emotional responses to doing things well can give you a quick snapshot of how you and your contentment are working together.

In the first column, write down five things you've done well recently, including simple things like going to bed on time or taking out the trash. In the second column, write down how you felt when you did those things well.

Things You've Done Well	Your Emotional Response(s)

If you see emotions other than contentment popping up here, turn to their sections to see what wisdom they're wanting to share with you.

Some Notes about Contentment

Many people have trouble with self-esteem and contentment simply because they don't know how to work with their shame. If you rarely feel content, or if you rarely feel proud of yourself, observe your relationship with shame. Do you struggle with a lot of unhealthy shaming messages? If so, see the sections on Shame and Burning Contracts. When your shame is freed from unhealthy and inauthentic messages, your contentment will soon be able to work naturally and appropriately.

Practices to Help You Work with Your Contentment

Empathic Mindfulness Practices: Grounding and Focusing ~ Defining Your Boundary ~ Burning Contracts ~ Renegotiating Contracts ~ Conscious Complaining (solo and with a partner) ~ Ethical Empathic Gossip ~ Rejuvenation

Additional Practices: Identifying your authentic values ~ Noticing the things you've done well ~ Working with your shame

It may be useful to circle the practices above that support your sense of contentment.

Personalizing Your Contentment Practices

Take a moment to feel into the contentment question: *How have I embodied my authentic values?*

It can be supportive to write down some of your most important values (such as loyalty, imagination, friendliness, etc.) as you learn to work with your contentment. Be prepared, however, to discover values that seem like yours but turn out to be inauthentic or imposed upon you by others. Feel free to strike through or erase values that don't belong to you (you can also use the Burning Contracts practice) and to replace them with values that are truly yours. Finding your authentic values and your authentic voice is a lifelong healing practice.

My Authentic Values

Joy: Affinity and Communion

The Gifts and Skills in Joy	Expansion ~ Communion ~ Inspiration Radiance ~ Splendor ~ Bliss
The Internal Questions for Joy	*What brings me deep connection and infinite expansion?* *How do I integrate this radiant experience?*
Some Nuances of Joy	**Soft Joy**: Encouraged, Inspired, Open, Peaceful **Medium Joy:** Excited, Expanded, Joyful, Ungrounded **Intense Joy:** Blissful, Euphoric, Manic, Overjoyed

JOY helps you feel a blissful sense of open-hearted communion and connection to others, to ideas, or to experiences. Joy is often treated as the queen of the emotions, or as a peak state to chase after and imprison. As you know by now, no emotion should be treated this way. Joy is a normal human emotion that has a specific purpose. Trying to capture or force your joy will create imbalances throughout your emotional ecosystem.

When you're working well with your joy, it will arise during moments of communion with nature, love, and beauty – when you feel as if you're one with everything. If you can recall the open and powerfully calm feelings you have when you're in your favorite natural setting at the most beautiful time of day, or when you're with a person or animal you love and trust completely, you'll be able to access your joy.

When you were little, how were you taught to treat joy?

What connects you to your joy today?

If joy is unavailable to you, what are some messages you've heard about joy? (See the earlier sections on Burning Contracts and Renegotiating Contracts if these messages are not supportive.)

Joy lives inside you; it's a natural human emotion, but we're usually taught to treat it as magical and unattainable. Thankfully, you can treat your joy with more respect. Welcome your joy when it arises, and let it recede when it's time to move on to other emotions. Flow is the key.

Some Notes about Joy

Joy is an expansive emotion that may lead you to drop your boundaries (your anger and shame) and open yourself to new experiences. In this openness, you may not require strong instincts (i.e., your fear), and you may be fairly unprotected. This is an important transition; sometimes you need to let go in order to soak up new experiences. However, make sure to ground and focus yourself afterward. Your other emotions – and your entire psyche – will need to reintegrate after extended periods of joy.

If you try to imprison joy, it can become exaggerated and unstable. When joy is unstable, it may intensify into mania, and it's important to be careful and aware – especially if your intense joy cycles with depression. Remember to seek help if your emotions are out of balance (see How Much Emotion Is Too Much? in part 4).

Also, joy can arise alongside grief because both emotions are involved in communion and connection. If you can allow yourself to grieve, joy will often arise in waves as you experience the deep and healing waters of grief.

Practices to Help You Work with Your Joy

Empathic Mindfulness Practices: Grounding and Focusing ~ Hands-On Grounding ~ Conscious Complaining (solo and with a partner) ~ Rejuvenation

Additional Practices: Being in nature ~ Connecting with those you love Surrounding yourself with beauty

It may be useful to circle the practices above that feel supportive to you and your joy.

Personalizing Your Joy Practices

Take a moment to feel into the joy questions: *What brings me deep connection and infinite expansion? How do I integrate this radiant experience?*

Many of us have been taught to treat joy as a magical peak state that should be chased down and imprisoned. This is silly, because joy is a natural human emotion that lives inside each of us. And thankfully, joy doesn't always have to be intense and overwhelming; you can experience it in simple ways.

Feel into your joy, and jot down some simple experiences that connect you to soft and medium states of joy, such as seeing a vibrant sunset, finding a lost item, laughing with close friends, and so forth. Come back to this page for reminders if you feel unable to access your joy.

PART 4

Support for Your Emotional Life

The following resources will help you nurture and
support your emotional skills and awareness.

How Much Emotion Is Too Much?

We've all been through times when one or more of our emotions was seemingly over-activated. Sometimes that activation is necessary: for instance, when you've got a huge amount of work to complete and your anxiety needs to be on task for weeks or months at a time.

In many circumstances, you can work with your active or repetitive emotions, rely on your Empathic Mindfulness practices, and channel those emotions skillfully. However, there are times when you'll need assistance with your emotions, and there are clear signs that will help you know when any emotion is too much.

When your emotions repeat continually and do not resolve, or when they overwhelm you or the people in your life, that's too much. It's time to find out what's going on.

Usually, your emotions will respond to you and resolve when you listen to them and channel them mindfully. But if you've got an emotion that repeats continually and will not resolve itself, no matter how many times you ask its questions or attend to the gifts and skills it brings to you, that's a clear sign that you could use some support.

 Does any emotion(s) feel like too much for you? If so, which emotion(s) is it?

a. Flip back to that emotion's section in this workbook. What gifts and skills does that emotion(s) bring to you?

b. Is the emotion(s) responding to a relevant situation in your life?

Is It the Emotion or the *Situation* That's Too Much?

If any highly activated or repetitive emotion is responding to an overwhelming or unhealthy situation in your life, then that emotion isn't too much; it's the *situation* that's too much, and your emotion is responding appropriately.

For instance, if anger is constantly activated in your life, and you know that it brings you the ability to identify what you value, set and restore proper boundaries, and maintain your sense of self, is there a clear reason for it to be activated so often? When you ask the anger questions – *What do I value?* and *What must be protected and restored?* – do you find boundary challenges or boundary violations that are constantly occurring? Does your anger have a good reason for appearing so frequently? Is it telling you something true? Is your anger trying to help you?

If so, you may need to reach out for support, not to fix your *emotion* but to address the troubling situation your emotion is responding to. When you can address the situation, your emotion(s) may be able to relax and stand down a bit.

When Your Emotions Need to Be Highly Activated

There are specific emotions that can become highly activated due to their nature. For instance, **anxiety** is a naturally active emotion that's focused on the future, and by its very nature, anxiety can unground you. It can also pull you out of the present moment as you focus on future tasks and deadlines.

If you don't yet have a practice for anxiety, and you don't realize that the presence of a sense of dread or danger means that **panic** is also present, you could easily become agitated or overwhelmed by these two powerful emotions, and you might need physical and therapeutic support to help your body and your emotions settle. Then, you can learn how to work with your anxiety and panic so that you'll be able to ground and focus yourself when these two essential emotions need to be on task.

Shame is another emotion that may become highly active and repetitive, either because you're repeating a behavior that isn't in alignment with your ethics, or because your shame is responding to outdated shaming messages that need the Burning Contracts and Renegotiating Contracts practices.

Situational depression, if it lasts too long, may settle into a soft form of depression called *dysthymia* or into major depression itself. If this happens, you'll need to reach out for support. Your **suicidal urge** may also become activated in this situation, and again, you'll need some support.

Joy can also cycle back and forth with a type of depression. This cycling joy is called *mania*, and it's a state to take seriously because joy naturally lowers your boundaries, ungrounds you, and reduces your access to the essential emotions in your fear family. You'll need to reach out for support if your joy is overactivated.

Frozen panic can also become cyclical and highly activated. Performing the healing actions (instead of the dubious ones) can help your body settle a bit, and finding a gentle somatic healing practice can also support you.

Anger can also become repetitive and activated (especially in men) when there's an underlying depressive condition. The anger can provide a boost of energy and sharp focus in the midst of the depressive condition, but the anger won't often track to any-thing identifiable. If you're dealing with constant and explosive anger, please reach out for support.

Relying on the Deep Wisdom of Your Emotions

In each of these cases, your emotions are intensified for important reasons. They're signaling that a problem exists, but *your emotions are not the problem*. You and they need support to identify and address the problem so that your emotions can get back to their regular work!

Because emotions are so powerful, a repetitive state may destabilize you, so attending to that emotion may require changes to your lifestyle (or therapeutic support) to help you understand and respond to the problems your emotions are highlighting.

You can also work with one of our licensed DEI consultants to engage directly with the emotion that became intensified or repetitive; it can tell you essential and even life-changing things about yourself and the world around you.

Take care of yourself, support the intelligence in your emotions, and listen closely to them so that you can take the healing actions they (and you) require. Emotions are irreplaceable, necessary, and powerfully wise. When they feel like too much, ask yourself, *Is it the emotion or is it the **situation** that's too much?*

Reflection Questions for Your Activated Emotions

 Which emotion is activated right now?

a. See that emotion's section in this workbook. What gifts does that emotion bring to you?

b. What are the questions for that emotion?

c. Are there any situations that are calling that emotion forward?

d. What kinds of support do you and your emotion need?

Your Personalized Practice for Your Activated Emotions

As you engage more directly with your emotions, you'll be able to track their flows over time. Observe the ones that tend to arise in their intense and activated states, and which situations bring them forward. See if you can find patterns in your emotional responses and write down the things that help you.

THE ACTIVATED EMOTION	THE SITUATION	WHAT HELPS?

Your Emotional Vocabulary List

A large and articulate emotional vocabulary can – all by itself – help you develop emotion-regulation skills. What's more, research is showing that a large emotional vocabulary can even protect your mental, physical, and emotional health!

My emotional vocabulary list is organized alphabetically by emotion and intensity level, and it has been crowd-sourced in my DEI community for more than a decade. Note that I've included words for the gifts, skills, and genius your emotions contain.

You can download this complete list (now in ten languages!) on my website at karlamclaren.com/emotional-vocabulary-page/. Enjoy building your vocabulary!

Personalizing Your Emotional Vocabulary List

Getting to Know Your Emotions: As you learn to work with your emotions, you can use this vocabulary list to help you identify what you're feeling (and at what level of activation). This is a simple way to learn about your emotional landscape and connect with your emotions.

Choosing Your Favorites: When we work with children, we have them choose their favorite vocabulary words as they learn to identify their emotions. You may enjoy writing down your own favorite words for your emotional states and keeping your personal vocabulary list where you can access it easily when you need to.

Playing with Nuance: If you have any emotions that come on very strongly, this list can help you learn how to identify your emotions when they're in their soft states. If you tend to leap into intensity with any emotion, learning about its soft state can help you identify the gifts it brings you, ask its questions, and tend to it earlier in its trajectory.

On the other hand, if there's an emotion that doesn't seem to be present for you, studying that emotion's soft vocabulary words and its gifts and skills may help you begin to track this more subtle emotion. Sometimes, you're already doing the work of one or more emotions (for instance, setting clear boundaries with your soft anger or connecting with your instincts and intuition with your soft fear). If so, those emotions may not actually need to appear in their medium *or* intense states very often!

Anger, Apathy, and Hatred		
Soft Anger, Apathy, Hatred	Medium Anger, Apathy, and Hatred	Intense Anger, Apathy, and Hatred
Ambivalent ~ Annoyed Assertive ~ Calm Certain Confident Crabby ~ Cranky Critical ~ Cross Detached ~ Determined Discerning ~ Disengaged Displeased ~ Distracted Frustrated ~ Honorable Impatient ~ Independent Irritated ~ Peeved Protective ~ Quiet Rankled ~ Secure Self-assured ~ Separate Steady ~ Uninspired	Affronted ~ Aggravated Angry ~ Antagonized Apathetic ~ Arrogant Autonomous ~ Aware of your shadow ~ Bored Bristling ~ Clear-eyed Cold ~ Courageous Defended ~ Dignified Disinterested Exasperated ~ Incensed Indifferent ~ Indignant Inflamed ~ Listless Mad ~ Offended Protected ~ Resentful Riled up ~ Sarcastic Self-aware ~ Sharp Sovereign ~ Steadfast Well boundaried	Aggressive ~ Appalled Belligerent ~ Bitter Contemptuous Disgusted ~ Energized Fierce ~ Furious Hateful ~ Hostile Hypocritical ~ Integrated Irate ~ Livid ~ Loathing Menacing ~ Numb Passionate ~ Piercingly aware ~ Powerful Projecting ~ Raging Ranting ~ Raving Righteous ~ Seething Shadow resourced Shielded ~ Spiteful Transformed ~ Tuned out Unresponsive ~ Vengeful Vicious ~ Vindictive Violent

Shame and Guilt

Soft Shame and Guilt	Medium Shame and Guilt	Intense Shame and Guilt
Awkward	Abashed ~ Apologetic	Belittled
Conscientious	Ashamed ~ Chagrined	Conscience-stricken
Considerate ~ Decent	Contrite ~ Culpable	Degraded ~ Demeaned
Discomfited ~ Ethical	Dignified ~ Embarrassed	Disgraced
Flushed ~ Flustered	Guilty ~ Honorable	Guilt-ridden
Forgiving ~ Hesitant	Humbled ~ Intimidated	Guilt-stricken
Honest ~ Humble	Just ~ Moral ~ Noble	Humiliated
Reserved ~ Restrained	Penitent ~ Principled	Incorruptible ~ Mortified
Self-conscious	Regretful ~ Remorseful	Ostracized ~ Projecting
	Reproachful	Righteous
	Respectable ~ Rueful	Self-condemning
	Self-effacing	Self-flagellating
	Self-respecting ~ Sheepish	Shamefaced
	Sorry ~ Speechless	Stigmatized
	Upstanding	
	Willing to change	
	Withdrawn	

Confusion

Soft Confusion	Medium Confusion	Intense Confusion
Adaptable ~ Changeable	Ambivalent ~ Bewildered	Befuddled
Doubtful ~ Innocent	Clouded ~ Confused	Discombobulated
Malleable	Contemplative ~ Floating	Disoriented ~ Escaping
Open-minded ~ Pensive	Fuzzy ~ Indecisive	Immobile ~ Lost
Preoccupied ~ Puzzled	Muddled ~ Nebulous	Mystified
Soft-focused	Perplexed ~ Spacious	Overwhelmed
	Uncertain ~ Unfocused	Scattered ~ Suspended
		Timeless ~ Waiting

Anxiety

Soft Anxiety	Medium Anxiety	Intense Anxiety
Capable ~ Clear-headed Focused ~ Organized Prepared	Activated ~ Anxious Attentive ~ Competent Conscientious ~ Deadline conscious ~ Efficient Energized ~ Excited Forward focused Motivated ~ Nervous Ready ~ Task focused Vigilant ~ Worried	Accomplished ~ Driven Frenzied Hyperactivated Laser focused Pressed ~ Vigorous

Fear and Panic

Soft Fear and Panic	Medium Fear and Panic	Intense Fear and Panic
Alert ~ Apprehensive Aware ~ Careful Cautious ~ Clear Concerned ~ Conscious Curious ~ Disconcerted Disquieted ~ Edgy Fidgety ~ Hesitant Insecure ~ Instinctive Intuitive ~ Leery ~ Lucid Mindful ~ Oriented Pensive ~ Perceptive Shy ~ Timid ~ Uneasy Watchful	Afraid ~ Alarmed Attentive ~ Aversive Distrustful ~ Disturbed Fearful ~ Focused Jumpy ~ Perturbed Rattled ~ Ready Resourceful Safety seeking ~ Shaky Startled ~ Suspicious Unnerved ~ Unsettled Vigorous ~ Wary	Dissociated Filled with dread Frenzied Healing from trauma Horrified Hyperactivated Immobile ~ Laser focused Motionless ~ Panicked Paralyzed ~ Petrified Phobic ~ Reintegrated Self-preserving ~ Shocked Survival focused Terrorized ~ Violent

Jealousy and Envy

Soft Jealousy and Envy	Medium Jealousy and Envy	Intense Jealousy and Envy
Concerned ~ Connected Disbelieving ~ Fair Insecure ~ Inspired Protective ~ Self-aware Trusting ~ Vulnerable Wanting	Ambitious ~ Amorous Bonded ~ Committed Covetous ~ Demanding Desirous ~ Devoted Disrespected Distrustful ~ Driven Envious ~ Equitable Generous ~ Guarded Jealous ~ Just ~ Lonely Loving ~ Loyal Motivated ~ Prosperous Romantic ~ Secure Self-preserving Threatened ~ Wary	Affluent ~ Ardent Avaricious ~ Deprived Fixated ~ Gluttonous Grasping ~ Greedy Green with envy Longing ~ Lustful Obsessed ~ Passionate Persistently jealous Possessive Power hungry Resentful ~ Voracious

Happiness, Contentment, and Joy

Soft Happiness, Contentment, and Joy	Medium Happiness, Contentment, and Joy	Intense Happiness, Contentment, and Joy
Amused ~ Calm Comfortable Encouraged ~ Engaged Friendly ~ Hopeful Inspired ~ Jovial ~ Naïve Open ~ Peaceful Smiling ~ Unaware Upbeat	Appreciative ~ Cheerful Confident ~ Contented Delighted ~ Excited Fulfilled ~ Glad Gleeful ~ Gratified Happy Healthy self-esteem Invigorated ~ Joyful Lively ~ Merry Optimistic ~ Playful Pleased ~ Praiseworthy Proud ~ Rejuvenated Tickled ~ Ungrounded Unrealistic	Arrogant ~ Awe filled Blissful ~ Ecstatic Egocentric ~ Elated Enthralled ~ Euphoric Exhilarated ~ Expansive Flighty ~ Giddy Gullible ~ Heedless Inflated ~ Jubilant Manic ~ Oblivious Overconfident Overjoyed ~ Radiant Rapturous ~ Reckless Renewed ~ Satisfied Self-aggrandized Thrilled

Sadness and Grief

Soft Sadness and Grief	Medium Sadness and Grief	Intense Sadness and Grief
Contemplative Disappointed Disconnected ~ Fluid Grounded ~ Listless Low ~ Steady ~ Regretful Relaxed ~ Releasing Restful ~ Wistful	Dejected ~ Discouraged Dispirited ~ Down Drained ~ Grieving Heavyhearted Honoring ~ Lamenting Melancholy ~ Mournful Rejuvenated ~ Relieved Remembering Respectful ~ Restored Sad ~ Soothed Sorrowful ~ Still ~ Weepy	Anguished ~ Bereaved Cleansed ~ Despairing Despondent ~ Forlorn Grief-stricken Heartbroken Inconsolable ~ Morose Released ~ Revitalized Sanctified

Depression and Suicidal Urges

Soft Depression and Suicidal Urges	Medium Depression and Suicidal Urges	Intense Depression and Suicidal Urges
Apathetic ~ Discouraged Disinterested ~ Dispirited Downtrodden ~ Fed up Feeling worthless ~ Flat Helpless ~ Humorless Impulsive ~ Indifferent Isolated ~ Lethargic Listless ~ Pessimistic Practical ~ Purposeless Realistic ~ Resolute Tired ~ Withdrawn World-weary	Bereft ~ Certain Constantly irritated, angry, or enraged (see the anger list above) Crushed ~ Depressed Desolate ~ Desperate Drained ~ Emancipated Empty ~ Fatalistic Gloomy ~ Hibernating Hopeless ~ Immobile Inactive ~ Inward focused Joyless ~ Miserable Morbid ~ Overwhelmed Passionless ~ Pleasureless Sullen	Agonized ~ Anguished Bleak ~ Death seeking Devastated ~ Doomed Freed ~ Frozen Gutted ~ Liberated Nihilistic ~ Numbed Reborn ~ Reckless Self-destructive ~ Suicidal Tormented ~ Tortured Transformed

A note about suicidal urges: If you're having any thoughts of suicide, don't wait until you're in the medium or intense states before you reach out for help. If you can identify your suicidal urges when they're soft, you can often stop yourself from falling into anguish or harming yourself.

When your suicidal urges appear in a soft state of (for instance) *pessimism* or *world-weariness*, you can ask, *What behavior or situation must end now? What can no longer be tolerated in my soul?* When the suicidal urge is in its soft state, you'll often be able to make the changes it requires without having to move into the intense states of (for instance) *torment* or *self-destructiveness*.

In the territory of the suicidal urge, your capacity for emotional awareness and sensitivity can literally save your life!

If you or anyone you know is feeling suicidal, free and confidential help is always available. Flip back to the Suicidal Urge section in this workbook to find lifeline services across the world.

Thank you for your emotional fluency and your willingness to reach out. Thank you for bringing more emotional awareness and empathy to our troubled world.

Your Nonspecific Emotion Words List

As you develop your emotional vocabulary, you may notice that many people don't have strong vocabularies or don't feel comfortable talking about emotions. Luckily, this doesn't need to stop you from developing your own emotional awareness and skills.

If people aren't able to identify or speak about emotions (or if they're disturbed or offended by the true names for emotions), you can use nonspecific words to gently bring awareness to the true emotion that's present. If you can frame your observation as a question (or use the phrase "It seems that you're feeling . . ."), you'll help people begin to develop their own emotional awareness and vocabulary.

We've found nine helpful and nonspecific emotion words, and three of them are almost magical because you can use them to describe nearly any emotion. They are *bad*, *stressed*, and *unhappy*. These are accepted ways to name most emotions, and they won't usually offend people.

Another three helpful words are *hurt*, *overwhelmed*, and *upset*. However, you may want to use these words carefully, because they suggest that a person is struggling or vulnerable, and many people don't want to admit that they ever feel that way. Use your best judgment.

There are also three words that many people use to avoid or hide their emotions: *fine*, *okay*, and *whatever*.

Notice how these nine words can be used to describe pretty much every emotion except happiness, contentment, and joy. That's stunning, but it explains why so many of us struggle to develop emotional awareness and emotional skills – both of which rely on a rich emotional vocabulary!

Use liberally: **Bad**, **Stressed**, and **Unhappy**

Use with care: **Hurt**, **Overwhelmed**, and **Upset**

Use when avoidance is wanted: **Fine**, **Okay**, and **Whatever** (people can use many other words to avoid emotions, of course!)

Take a moment to write down some gentle phrases or questions you could ask when people are clearly feeling emotions but are unable (or unwilling) to name them. It's important not to name other people's emotions for them (that's a boundary violation) but instead to create a welcoming space where they can begin to identify their own emotional states.

Thank you for creating a space for more emotional awareness in our waiting world, even when it needs to be nonspecific awareness!

Resources

As you move forward in your emotional awareness adventure, these resources will support you, your emotions, your empathy, your relationships, and your healing.

Supportive Websites

EMPATHY ACADEMY: empathyacademy.org

This Dynamic Emotional Integration (DEI) online community and learning site is a wonderful place to continue your exploration of your emotions and your empathy. You can join our community space or take courses on emotions, empathy, the Empathic Mindfulness practices, art, movement, self-care, and communication. You can also find and work with licensed DEI trainers and consultants across the globe and learn about the DEI licensing program.

HELP GUIDE: helpguide.org

This site offers excellent free support and information about mental and psychological conditions, and it does so in a welcoming and nonalarmist way. This site helps you understand your (or others') conditions and see a clear way forward.

KARLA MCLAREN: karlamclaren.com

My site is full of information, tons of free stuff, and resources, including card decks, reference guides, pocket-sized emotional vocabulary lists, and all of my books and audio learning programs. My blog also contains further information on each of the emotions, on my Six Essential Aspects of Empathy model, and on whatever I happen to be interested in at the moment!

Emotional Health and Well-Being

Barrett, Lisa Feldman. *How Emotions Are Made: The Secret Life of the Brain*. New York: Houghton Mifflin Harcourt, 2017.

Devine, Megan. *It's OK That You're Not OK: Meeting Grief and Loss in a Culture That Doesn't Understand*. Boulder, CO: Sounds True, 2017.

Dodes, Lance. *The Heart of Addiction: A New Approach to Understanding and Managing Alcoholism and Other Addictive Behaviors*. New York: HarperCollins, 2002.

Hecht, Jennifer Michael. *The Happiness Myth: Why What We Think Is Right Is Wrong*. New York: HarperOne, 2007.

Hochschild, Arlie Russell. *The Managed Heart: Commercialization of Human Feeling*. Berkeley: University of California Press, 2003.

Lamia, Mary. *Understanding Myself: A Kid's Guide to Intense Emotions and Strong Feelings*. Washington, DC: Magination Press, 2010.

———. *What Motivates Getting Things Done: Procrastination, Emotions, and Success*. Lanham, MD: Rowman & Littlefield, 2018.

Lerner, Harriet. *Why Won't You Apologize? Healing Big Betrayals and Everyday Hurts*. New York: Gallery Books, 2017.

McLaren, Karla. *The Language of Emotions: What Your Feelings Are Trying to Tell You*. Boulder, CO: Sounds True, 2023.

Shadow Work

Bly, Robert. *A Little Book on the Human Shadow*. San Francisco: HarperSanFrancisco, 1988.

Brinton Perera, Sylvia. *The Scapegoat Complex: Toward a Mythology of Shadow and Guilt*. Toronto: Inner City Books, 1983.

Johnson, Robert. *Owning Your Own Shadow: Understanding the Dark Side of the Psyche*. San Francisco: HarperSanFrancisco, 1993.

Zweig, Connie, and Jeremiah Abrams, eds. *Meeting the Shadow: The Hidden Power of the Dark Side of Human Nature*. New York: Tarcher/Putnam, 1991.

Trauma Healing

Bonanno, George. *The End of Trauma: How the New Science of Resilience Is Changing How We Think about PTSD*. New York: Basic Books, 2021.

de Becker, Gavin. *The Gift of Fear: And Other Survival Signals That Protect Us from Violence*. New York: Dell, 1999.

Levine, Peter. *Healing Trauma: A Step-by-Step Program for Restoring the Wisdom of the Body* (online course). Boulder, CO: Sounds True, 2011.

McGonigal, Kelly. *The Upside of Stress: Why Stress Is Good for You, and How to Get Good at It*. New York: Avery, 2015.

About the Author

KARLA MCLAREN, M.Ed., is an award-winning author, educator, workplace consultant, and social science researcher. She developed the first-ever grand unified theory of emotions that uncovers the genius in the emotional realm and classifies emotions in terms of how they function, what forms of intelligence they contain, and how to work with them directly. She is the founder and CEO of Emotion Dynamics Inc., and the developer of the Empathy Academy online learning community.

Her applied work, Dynamic Emotional Integration® (also known as DEI), revalues even the most "negative" emotions and opens startling new pathways into self-awareness, effective communication, and healthy empathy. Licensed DEI professionals are available across the globe and can be found at empathyacademy.org.

DEI also incorporates Karla's groundbreaking Six Essential Aspects of Empathy model, which highlights all of the processes in healthy empathy and makes them clearly understandable, accessible, and manageable for everyone.

Karla is the author of many books in a dozen languages, including *The Language of Emotions: What Your Feelings Are Trying to Tell You*, *The Power of Emotions at Work: Accessing the Vital Intelligence in Your Workplace*, *Embracing Anxiety: How to Access the Genius Inside This Vital Emotion*, and *The Art of Empathy: A Complete Guide to Life's Most Essential Skill*.

Karla lives with her beloved family in Northern California, where she volunteers as the donations coordinator for Sonoma County Acts of Kindness, a small but mighty anarchist nonprofit that does direct street outreach and advocacy to support unsheltered folks.

About Sounds True

SOUNDS TRUE was founded in 1985 by Tami Simon with a clear mission: to disseminate spiritual wisdom. Since starting out as a project with one woman and her tape recorder, we have grown into a multimedia publishing company with a catalog of more than 3,000 titles by some of the leading teachers and visionaries of our time, and an ever-expanding family of beloved customers from across the world.

In more than three decades of evolution, Sounds True has maintained our focus on our overriding purpose and mission: to wake up the world. We offer books, audio programs, online learning experiences, and in-person events to support your personal growth and awakening, and to unlock our greatest human capacities to love and serve.

At SoundsTrue.com you'll find a wealth of resources to enrich your journey, including our weekly *Insights at the Edge* podcast, free downloads, and information about our nonprofit Sounds True Foundation, where we strive to remove financial barriers to the materials we publish through scholarships and donations worldwide.

To learn more, please visit SoundsTrue.com/freegifts or call us toll-free at 800.333.9185.

Together, we can wake up the world.